The Way of Mary

Following Her Footsteps Toward God

MARY FORD-GRABOWSKY

PARACLETE PRESS

BREWSTER, MASSACHUSETTS

The Way of Mary: Following Her Footsteps Toward God

2007 First Printing

Copyright © 2007 by Mary Ford-Grabowsky

ISBN: 978-1-55725-522-8

Library of Congress Cataloging-in-Publication Data
Ford-Grabowsky, Mary.
  The way of Mary: following her footsteps toward God / by
Mary Ford-Grabowsky.
      p. cm.
  Includes bibliographical references (p.   ) and index.
  ISBN 978-1-55725-522-8 (alk. paper)
  1. Mary, Blessed Virgin, Saint--Prayers and devotions. I. Title.
BX2160.23.F67 2007
232.91--dc22   2007034938

10 9 8 7 6 5 4 3 2 1

Published by Paraclete Press
Brewster, Massachusetts
www.paracletepress.com

Printed in the United States of America

FOR

Christian Louis Potts,

"flame of love."

Thank you with all my heart for your adorable joy,
soul beauty, and sacred teachings about everyone and everything.
I love you.

CONTENTS

 PREFACE

IN 1994, MY HUSBAND AND I SPENT AN AMAZING WEEK IN
GUATEMALA with our daughter Tara, a medical student who
was working in Guatemala City that summer in a hospital
for the poor. Friends of hers recommended a visit to a
"charming" village virtually unknown to tourists at the
time: Chichicastenango. We rented an ancient Jeep for
the drive up a wildly winding mountain road that was
continually punctuated by giant potholes and deep ruts.
Today it is a beautifully paved road, but on that day, I tried
to avert my eyes from thousand-foot drops at every turn
as we crashed into and out of a dozen ruts and eventually
arrived at the top, totally unprepared for the breathtaking
beauty all around us.

On one side, an ocean of Mayans dressed in bright blue
and red were gathered for market day. On the other side,
an alluring path led us to what appeared to be a tiny white
church built on top of an ancient pyramid. At the top of
the stairs, a very old Mayan *brujo* (healer) with a saintly face
and stooped shoulders was gently swinging incense over
a crippled woman, softly chanting in his native Quiché
what were unmistakably prayers. After a few minutes, the
woman left, and the *brujo,* with an air of infinite peace
and humility, opened the small doors of the church and

humbly stationed himself at the back. People who looked very poor and very ill waited in a long line for him.

Through the opened doors I saw in the semi-darkness a long row of burning white candles running the length of the center aisle floor, which was thickly covered with fresh flower petals. The beauty was beyond anything I had ever seen. My daughter and I tiptoed into the church and sat down on a side bench to be as unobtrusive as possible. I immediately felt myself saturated in love. The whole room was full of love. The air was rich and dense and luminous, like velvet. I noticed beside me at the end of our bench a statue of Mary, unusually compelling in a tasteful combination of Mayan and Christian dress. It had a strong spiritual presence, as works of art portraying Mary often do, and I recited the Hail Mary. Everything seemed to slow down and stop. I could feel myself sinking deeper and deeper into beauty, into holiness. Before long, I lost track of time and even of myself.

My daughter nudged me, pointing to her watch. A half hour had gone by, and we had to check into the hotel. Reluctantly, I stood up to leave. Many years of prayer and meditation had given me wondrous experiences, spiritual and mystical, but the depths of love in this sacred place, this divine womb, surpassed everything. Still enveloped in love, I listened to the Mayan's tender chanting for the poorest of the poor, then looked back at Mary, thinking about the power that she (and he) exuded.

Two days later, we drove down the mountain early for an appointment with a surgeon who would tell me the fate of a finger on my right hand. It had been nearly severed a few days earlier when a huge wrought-iron door had slammed on it, and it was not healing. The skin had turned black; the graft was not taking; and the doctor was not optimistic.

Suddenly I realized I had missed a once-in-a-lifetime opportunity to ask a powerful, obviously revered Mayan *brujo* to pray for me. I shook my head, wondering how I could have been in the holiest situation of my life and not ask for help when it was such an obvious thing to do. Apparently I was so lost in the love and beauty there that it was impossible to think of myself.

A few hours later, the surgeon unbandaged my hand and exclaimed, "How did you do *that*?" I looked down and saw that the finger looked alive again. The wound was healed. "Oh, I have a great surgeon!" I replied, laughing, too shocked to say anything meaningful. He responded with a tone of surprising gravity: "*I* did not do that. I don't have that kind of power."

Today as I write these words, I look down at the fine scar encircling my fingertip and remember the riches of love emanating from an ancient Mayan healer so poor that he burned his sacred incense in a rusty tin can. He was the most humble person I have ever been blessed to encounter, and my scar, like a little halo that I imagine shining over his head, will always symbolize for me the mysterious love of God at work in humankind, the great mystery of Christ in us. It keeps me aware of the death-and-rebirth cycles that accumulate over the course of a lifetime, and of the ultimate truth of Christian resurrection faith.

Through the years since then, my daughter, who is now a doctor, has told me about many minor miracles like my own and others much more powerful that she has witnessed in the hospital and that no one can explain. She says that friends always ask her what was her most exciting, horrifying, or bloody experience in the hospital. She wishes they would ask her what experience was the holiest.

Thinking about that day in Chichicastenango, I can feel again the inexplicable spiritual impact of the statue of Mary, the strong feminine presence and loveliness it portrayed. I have often visited the Cloisters in New York City to enjoy medieval statues of Mary that I love, but this one was different: she seemed to step out of it and come alive. Although I did not have a particular devotion to her at that time, something had moved me to recite the Hail Mary. It was not a conscious prayer for my injury to heal, yet there was undeniably a relationship between the powerful impression she had on me, the unbelievable beauty of the Mayan healer, the love he generated in the little church, and the renewed flesh on my hand. Apparently the beauty of spiritual presence had opened my heart, and life-giving grace had flowed in.

This book originated in that experience, and the only point of my retelling it here is to wish you and your loved ones similar healing, or whatever you need that only God can give.

PART ONE

Toward a New Spirituality of Mary

CHAPTER 1
A Sacred Pilgrimage with Mary

ALL OVER THE WORLD, GLORIOUS POETRY, STAINED GLASS WINDOWS, SCULPTURES, SHRINES, AND BREATHTAKING CHAPELS have been created by artists such as Matisse, Chagall, and Michelangelo to glorify Mary and honor her memory. Where people are poor, colorful rituals honoring Mary on her Holy Days imprint the bleak cycle of the year with excitement, meaning, and joy.[1] In Eastern Orthodoxy, thousands of icons of Mary are often said to shine with the beauty of the divine energies. In the twelfth century alone, more than fifty soaring cathedrals in the new Gothic style were named for Mary, and to this day they draw millions of tourists each year to feast spiritually on the heart-stopping grandeur of a Chartres or a Notre Dame. Throughout the world, music composed for Mary and images of the Madonna brighten the darkness like living lights.

How many millions of Hail Marys and rosaries are said every day? Estimates vary from millions to billions, but it is said more than any other prayer from the vast global Christian treasury. Each year, some twelve million women and men make pilgrimages to Our Lady of Guadalupe in Mexico alone, and countless millions more travel to Marian shrines all over the world.

Muslims revere Mary more than any other woman in history and regard her as a prophet. An entire chapter in the Qur'an is devoted to her, and many mosques offer prayer niches in the eastern corner that are dedicated to Mary. Devout Muslims make pilgrimages to Marian shrines in the Middle East and all over the world to pray and be with her.

Among the great Eastern religions, Buddhism for much of its 2,500 years and Hinduism for well over 3,000 years have abounded with adored female figures, wise and saintly. Some are *bodhisattvas,* who renounce salvation until everyone has been saved. But there is no single female figure in any religion comparable to Mary. Long before the council of Ephesus formally exalted her with the title of *Theotokos* (Mother of God) in 431, Mary was the most beautiful rising star on the horizon of human history. Today she is more loved and revered, more represented in art and ritual, than any other woman who ever lived on earth. Indeed, some people worship Mary as though she were God the Mother, rather than the Mother of God.

In addition to these many forms of veneration, we should honor Mary also as a mother of a human child who grew up at her side, receiving her love and tender care.

This book invites you on a sacred pilgrimage with Mary that celebrates both her historical life on earth two thousand years ago and her momentous influence on the human heart ever since. *The Way of Mary* gives you an opportunity to delve into your own spirituality and grow in self-discovery and self-understanding while moving closer to Mary in prayer. The pilgrimage, which you can make in fourteen consecutive days or at as leisurely a pace as you like, is based on fourteen of the most beautiful and moving New Testament stories in which Mary can be seen to play a vibrant, inspiring role. While this book dwells on Mary, the mother of Jesus, as a model for us, she is implicitly present on every page as the heavenly woman clothed in the sun with stars in her hair (Revelation 12:1), who always hears human prayers.

This book helps to bring to the surface a great underground river of love and trust that has flowed from Mary like divine grace since shortly after her death. Although the book is carefully based in Scripture and Mariology, it speaks in the language of love, not dogma. Leaving aside discussions of ontology, this book limns Mary in her full and deep human holiness, beauty, joy, and grief. Her spirit is always held high toward God, as though her soul were drenched in some special strength and grace, even in times of life's hardest realities. Rumi, the master mystical poet of Persia, explains in an exquisite poem, translated by Coleman Barks, how Mary gracefully bears the unbearable, such as the execution of her precious son:

> Like . . . a rose as it opens, she leaped, as her habit was, out of herself into the Presence.

Mary not only embodies the loftiest spiritual potential in human beings as well as the very strengths and virtues we most value and want to realize in daily life, she also leads the life of affection that we all long to lead. And *she believes*. Nothing can extinguish her faith. As a number of Christian writers have observed, and secular journalists have echoed in publications such as *Time, Life, Newsweek*, and *The Economist*, Mary is the image of everything a woman or a man could hope to be. It is this whole and gracious Mary to whom I hope you will draw closer in this book: Mary, the radiant exemplar and living archetype; the one-woman model of everything we cherish and long to be.

THE WAY OF MARY

Here are the 14 steps of *The Way of Mary*:

1. The Annunciation:
    Mary agrees to become the mother of Jesus.
    (Luke 1:26–38)
2. The Visit to Elizabeth:
    Mary visits her cousin Elizabeth while both women are waiting to give birth. (Luke 1:39–45)
3. The Magnificat:
    Mary sings her great song of praise, "My soul magnifies the Lord and my spirit rejoices in God my savior." (Luke 1:46–55)
4. The Nativity:
    Mary gives birth to Jesus in Bethlehem. (Luke 2:1–7)

5. Pondering Things in Her Heart:
   Mary thinks deeply about profound events. (Luke 2:19, 51)

6. Simeon's Prophecy:
   A sword will pierce Mary's heart. (Luke 2:25–35)

7. Meeting the Prophet Anna:
   A woman prophet proclaims the greatness of Mary's son.
   (Luke 2:36–38)

8. The Escape to Egypt:
   Mary and Joseph become political refugees to save
   Jesus from Herod's killings. (Matthew 2:13–23)

9. Finding Her Missing Son:
   Mary finds her twelve-year-old son debating with
   learned men. (Luke 2:41–51)

10. The Wedding at Cana:
    Mary intervenes to help inaugurate her son's public
    ministry. (John 2:1–11)

11. At the Cross:
    Mary stands at the foot of the cross with her sister,
    Mary the wife of Clopas, the beloved disciple John,
    and Mary Magdalene. (John 19:25)

12. Jesus speaks to Mary from the cross:
    Mary becomes the spiritual mother of all disciples for
    all time. (John 19:26–27)

13. Waiting for the Spirit:
    Mary prays with the disciples in the Upper Room for
    the Spirit of Christ to come. (Acts 1:12–14)

14. Pentecost:
    The Spirit of Mary's Son brings sacred gifts of
    wisdom and speech. (Acts 2:1–4)

Each of these fourteen steps contains a wide variety of spiritual practices, ranging from methods for entering silence to activities that enliven the mind and warm the heart. Among the practices are meditations, reflections, and ancient and modern prayers. There are also visualizations, artwork, mantras, and ideas for freeing the creative spirit. These practices reflect the spirit of the East in addition to the spirit of the West, bringing together the most effective and sacred purposes of Christian, Hindu, Buddhist, and Sufi spiritualities. The results are powerful. Ultimately, *The Way of Mary* seeks to nurture the seed of Christ at the ground of the soul, just as Mary, when she was raising Jesus, nourished the deep identity concealed in him. Who better than the mother of the Christ can bring up and nurture Christlike women and men? Everyone touched by her love discovers the strengths and energies and illumined beauty of the soul.

The steps are arranged in chronological order according to Mary's age, beginning when at about fourteen she was invited to become the mother of a son with a world-shattering destiny. Subsequent steps trace her life through ordinary and extraordinary events, all biblically based, until the age of about forty-seven, when the Spirit of her Son descended on Pentecost in about the year 33. After that we have no reliable information, although unverifiable traditions situate her in Jerusalem or in Ephesus (in modern-day Turkey) with the beloved disciple, John, or at home in Nazareth for an unknowable number of years. Enchanting legends and lovely works of art depict many versions of Mary's death, but, sadly, nothing reliable has yet been learned about it.

The Way of Mary uses traditional dates for Jesus' and Mary's lives, although they are not historically accurate since we do not know the precise year when Jesus was born. This book calls the year of his birth 1 and the year of his death 33, although he may have been born several years earlier or later, and gives fourteen as Mary's age at the Annunciation, although she may have been thirteen. In the interest of simplicity, all other dates are calculated on the basis of these two.[2]

TEACHING HER FUTURE TEACHER

How do you raise your child, how do you interact with him, if he is also the Son of God, the Messiah of your people? That question must have always been present in Mary's mind, in one form or another, from the moment of the Annunciation. And as you watch your baby become a boy with prodigious spiritual and intellectual gifts, and you see more and more clearly that he has been called to history's most extreme religious challenge, how do you teach good manners and correct his grammar, as loving mothers do? It must be almost impossible to understand that one's child is the long-awaited Savior, even though Mary is told many times either explicitly or implicitly who Jesus is: first by Gabriel, the angel sent to invite her participation in redemption; and then by the prophet Simeon at the time of Jesus' presentation in the temple when he was forty days old. On that same day, the prophet Anna recognized who Jesus was. There is no question, of course, that Mary believed her boy was more God's son than her own; nevertheless, it was a question of being the only woman ever asked to do so much.

To say the least, it is uncomfortable to imagine Jesus' uneducated mother teaching her future teacher, but the truth is, a mother is inevitably her child's teacher, and her influence on him goes deep and lasts for a lifetime. Like all mothers-to-be, since the beginning of time and in every corner of the earth, Mary undoubtedly discussed the situation with her beloved cousin Elizabeth while they waited together for the birth of their sons, with her own mother, and perhaps with a sister and her grandmother, too. As the loving wife of a wise and sensitive man, she unquestionably discussed over and over again with Joseph the great issues of raising this holy child.

When Jesus was twelve, and his parents found him in the temple debating with learned men, it became apparent that he knew who he was. But it seems likely that mother and son had discussed this fact frequently and long before the temple episode.

How then to bring him up? Probably, when he was a baby and a toddler, she treated him with the same love and patience and forbearance that mothers innately have for their children. She bathed and swaddled him, fed him and sewed for him. She fixed and kissed his scratches and scrapes. She tenderly cared for him and was always present for her son. As Jesus grew older, she showed him how to feed himself, how to be well-mannered at meals and respectful of elders, how to behave with other children. Perhaps ingrained admiration for his mother led to the respect for women that he exhibited throughout his life, even daring to speak with a woman at a well, although the law forbade men to have public converse with women. Probably by her example as much as by her words, Mary taught her son to reflect before acting, to ponder things in his heart before making decisions.

What was it like when Jesus turned three or four, and his uniqueness began to be more and more noticeable? Was it a little like being the mother of Mozart, although in some indescribably greater manner, when little Mozart at the age of five composed the *Andante in C*? Mozart's mother had education to help her understand, while Mary was illiterate. But Mary surpassed all women of all time in insight, wisdom, and faith. She could educate her son through the psalms she sang to him and the Bible stories that Jewish mothers of her era usually knew by heart. Probably she expanded and explicated these stories to evoke insights and original thinking in her child. Perhaps she helped open his mind to the wonder of thinking and speculating and imagining.

Surely she taught him her beliefs and trust and faith in God. Especially important in Jesus' learning process was his mother's constant encouragement. She imbued him with her own *gravitas*, her quiet strength of character. She taught him to be responsible, most likely by example, but also by correcting him when he failed to live up to her standards and expectations. For instance, when he failed to meet the caravan after Passover and instead sat and debated with temple scholars, she rebuked him with a soft anger born of a worried mother's concern.

She helped him recognize injustice, as she herself had expressed it at the age of fourteen in her powerful Magnificat, and she showed him that it is right to feel angry about injustice and to battle it wherever it occurs. It would be many years before Jesus overturned money lenders' tables at the back of the temple, but perhaps there was a seed of his mother's teachings in that emotional moment. Somehow, probably because of her strong Jewish family tradition—all the convictions, experiential knowledge, and wisdom passed from generation to generation—Mary was able to teach Jesus to confront the power of others, be it spiritual, physical, or military, without fear and with inner calm and faith. How many times did she tell him Bible stories such as that of David and Goliath or Daniel in the Lion's Den?

We do not know exactly why God chose Mary to be the mother of the Messiah, but it seems fair to assume that her mind and spirit and soul reflected what God wanted to see in his Son. A loving mother has a vast impact on her child.

The mother of Jesus was willing to spend and be spent in the journey of raising her child, and she is willing to do the same for us. Entering into a relationship with her by practicing the steps in this book is to learn for yourself that "there is no limit to the holiness one can attain through closeness to Mary."[3]

While Jesus nurtures human spirituality through unforgettable sayings and stories, his mother inspires us less through words than through her actions and the essence of who she is. While Mary's ultimate meaning and the reasons for our fascination with her have to do with her place in heaven at the side of her son and with her significant role in redemption, her earthly life holds immense importance as a model for our own. Mary is the very picture of our human potentials and possibilities, and she left us a path that we can follow.

She is a wisdom teacher, a teacher by example who excites the spiritual imagination as no other woman ever has, inspiring women and men across time to follow her path of transforming love. Of all the words spoken by women preserved in the entire history of writing for well over three thousand years, probably nothing has been as studied and cherished generation after generation as Mary's song of praise, the Magnificat: "My soul magnifies the Lord, and my spirit rejoices in God my savior...." Her outburst of joy has incomparably rich meaning for women, since it originates in Mary's greeting to her cousin Elizabeth, when the two women were waiting to give birth. Meeting at such a sacred time of life, they bonded immediately and deeply, as women from time immemorial have tended to do.

The Mother of Jesus is the exemplar of all human lives, men's as well as women's. In essence, Mary shows us all how to *be*: how to be a believer; how to be waiting for the Spirit; how to be in grief and happiness, in the face of mystery, in relationship to other people, in relationship to God. And she has much to teach us also about *doing*, in the sense of doing the right thing at the right time for the right purposes. For example, when she took charge at Cana, she turned around a downward spiral of events and helped to inaugurate her son's public ministry. Scholars have barely begun to grasp the enormity of her proactive stance and decisive actions on that day.

Sally Cunneen, the author of the book *In Search of Mary*, explains why she models her life on Mary's:

> [Mary] is a genuine model to me now as she was not when I was young. As a pregnant mother and as witness to the cross, she testifies to the joy, the pain, and the promise of all human life. She unites the power of what early centuries saw in her as "male" virtue with the demanding human virtue of compassion. Above all, she reminds me of God's insistence that all creation and every human being, no matter how poor or powerless, is truly significant. How could that message be sent more pointedly than by the story of the son of God born in a stable to a poor woman? Yesterday, today, and tomorrow, the image of Mary calls on us to be strong and creative in our responses to the sacred potentialities of all life.[4]

Ultimately, Mary is a model of how to live. One of the holiest and most human instances of this occurred at the Annunciation, when she was invited to give birth to

Jesus. How better to show us the way than through her positive, welcoming response to the greatest challenge with which any woman has ever been presented? She knew it could not be easy or always joyful to be the mother of the Messiah, nor was it easy to find her voice when she finally spoke. On the contrary, it took tremendous courage to lift up her heart in trust and agree to an overwhelming destiny.

Mary's response to Gabriel was simple, yet majestic and overflowing with humble confidence in herself and in her God: "Let it be." That is all she said. Yet these words have become a hallmark for Christians because they speak volumes about her inherent wisdom—and the spiritual potential in every human heart. This example alone of the way Mary is and what she does is enough to explain her role as the outstanding female model of all time, a beautiful and powerful star who outshines the world's entire heritage of queens, heroines, and goddesses.

Let us thank God that Mary shines over the sea of the soul. Let us pray with Pope John Paul II, who loved Mary and dedicated his life to her: *Totus tuus,* "all yours." Mary, I am all yours.

CHAPTER 2
A Path We Can Follow

Before we turn to the steps on *The Way of Mary*, let us consider some areas that will aid us in our journey. Familiarity with these will prepare us for what comes in the steps.

FREEING THE SPIRITUAL INTELLECT

A beautiful painting of Mary by Georges de La Tour called *The Education of the Virgin* (now in the Frick Collection in New York) portrays Mary as a young student absorbed in book learning under the tutelage of her mother. Light pours from Mary's face, and she holds a candle in her hand, hinting at the illumination she both brings to and receives from her education. Of course, in real life, neither Mary nor her mother would have received any formal education, but de La Tour's radiant scene depicts Mary convincingly as being deep in thought while her eyes shine with love, and she is clearly very close to God. Today we would call the remarkable attribute that de La Tour makes visible her great spiritual intellect.

In Mary, the spiritual intellect is free and active in everyday life, as it can be in us.

One of the Christian mystics remarked, "See how our eyes shine when we talk about God." The more we converse in the family or in our community or with friends about divine things, the more we develop our spiritual intellect. The more we look, the more we are able to see. The more we pray and search for God's holiness in everything and everyone, the closer we come to having a clear and open mind that, like Mary's, reflects the light of God.

THE SACRED FEMININE

It is in part because of Mary's perfect embodiment of the feminine and her vast richness of female experience that art, music, literature, and history have perpetuated her story, generation after generation, for two millennia. Today's electronic media show clearly that no other woman has ever been as revered, loved, and prayed to as she.

The New Testament depicts Mary's femininity in many stories, and they are all reimagined and retold in this book over the course of the fourteen steps. For example, her meeting with Elizabeth on Day 2 of the pilgrimage records deep feelings of intimacy and joy in another woman's company. Day 3, still with Elizabeth, shows the feminine ease of connectedness. At Cana on Day 10, her profoundly felt compassion and caring save a newly married bride and groom from embarrassment. On Day 1, the power of female intuition helps Mary say yes at the Annunciation. In the Upper Room on Day 13, when she prays with the disciples for the Spirit of Christ to come, her capacity to wait evokes thousands of years of women waiting: waiting for the right partner, waiting for a sick person to heal or for a dying person to die, waiting for a husband to return, waiting for a child to be born, waiting for the children to come home from school, waiting for a daughter to leave home to marry, waiting to sew the final thread in a beautiful quilt of life.

It is especially significant that Days 1 through 4, almost a third of the pilgrimage, are concerned with the miracle and wonder of the female body, conceiving and growing a child inside, giving birth, and feeding the baby milk made inside herself. It is important to realize, however, that the uniquely feminine imagery of pregnancy and all that it entails applies not only to women who become mothers. It applies as fully to all other women and also to all men, because it symbolizes the fullness of the divine in Mary—precisely as it symbolizes the indwelling of Christ in ourselves.

THINKING WITH LOVE

When something profound occurred in Mary's life, when an event was amazing, mysterious, confusing, or painful, she turned inward to consider it contemplatively in the silence of God. It is likely that she trained herself when she was very young to pause and turn inward to search for the truth and understand the experience before speaking or reacting, before reaching conclusions, or before making a superficial response.[5] It is as though she wanted, first, to drink from the soul's inner well of wisdom that transforms ordinary human behavior into a spiritual act. So you will find as you follow *The Way of Mary* that there is a moment of spiritual surrender between an experience and her response to it that creates enormous interior space for not only grace to enter, but also God's love. A poem about Mary by the masterful poet Rumi speaks movingly about these kinds of issues. In the poem, he imagines Mary at the Incarnation, confronting Gabriel's frightening surprise with great holiness, saying to herself before she replies to the angel: "I'll hide inside God." This is a beautiful example of *thinking with love,* and Rumi, like hundreds of Christian saints, urges us to do the same, to be like Mary, to say what Mary said, to think and speak lovingly.

Another example of *thinking with love* comes from a non-Christian friend who gave me the following account of a meeting he attended with the Dalai Lama:

> The Dalai Lama was in a conference with five people when a monk interrupted to give him a message. The Dalai Lama wept for several minutes, then informed the group that the previous night, Chinese soldiers had tortured and killed 120 Tibetan monks and nuns. He finished by bowing his head and saying, "Now let us pray for the Chinese."

If you have explored the rooms of your soul with a reliable spiritual guide, you may have perceived a beauty in the soul that is mellow, like candlelight at dusk. Mary radiates this loveliness as no one else, and she can bring it out in ourselves. Emulate her way of *thinking with love,* and she will be there in your striving.

THINKING WITH FAITH

The difference between secular thinking and Mary's way of thinking is not only love: it is also faith. *Thinking with faith* allowed her, as it does us, to look forward to the future with joy and to grow old without anxiety. Mary is a believer who teaches us through her example to cultivate an attitude of trust and to bring thoughts full of trusting words to everything we say and do. There is a deeper dimension to everything, and that is what faith sees. Many people who fail to look for meaning beneath the surface, beneath the obvious, carry a burden of heavy suffering, like the famous Hollywood actress who attributed her tormented life to the fact that, as she put it, "Everywhere I go, I take me with me." In unforgettably poignant contrast, the mystic Nicolas of Cusa said,

Wherever I turn, You are there.[6]

In the same spirit, a C.S. Lewis novel features a lovely archdeacon who observes at each new experience, "This, too, art Thou."

Thinking with faith has amazing spiritual results that Mary illustrates at every step of our pilgrimage with her, and the beautiful traits that we see in her are all in our own souls waiting to be released.

If you are following *The Way of Mary* for the first time, pray in the morning to remember to look beneath the surface for God's activity within your experience, and thank God at night that you did. Or take up the modest but powerful practice of Andal, India's great woman poet from the eighth century:

> Three times each day,
> I invoke Your Name in prayer.[7]

BEING WITH JOY

Take five minutes to be with a happy infant or toddler, and you are sure to experience joy, the child's *and* your own. You might see the baby's face light up when he catches sight of a mobile, or a toddler's whole body wiggle with delight when she is lifted onto a swing. We feel their joy because it is a natural soul quality that springs up spontaneously and leaps contagiously from one being to another, like laughter. How much more fervently must Mary—the mother of the Lord Jesus Christ—have rejoiced in the light on Jesus' tiny face when he smiled for the first time? Not only did she share the bliss of any mother nursing, cuddling, and singing to her child, but also she was the only woman ever to know the blessing of birthing and raising the Son of God. Her heart must have soared at times to the most sublime rapture and exultation.

Mary is the Mother of Sorrow, but we should think of her also as the Mother of Joy. She conversed with Jesus Christ in the family home throughout his boyhood, adolescence, and young manhood. She saw spiritual powers emerge in him and evolve miraculously. She must have wondered and delighted at his quest for learning and for closeness to God.

And there were other areas of joyousness. As a family member, neighbor, and friend, Mary attended wedding parties, celebrations, and religious feasts, where she enjoyed, like all human beings, the earthy pleasures of good friendship, food, and wine. She enjoyed the blessings of traveling—sometimes with the nuclear family; at other times in a large caravan with extended family and friends; and sometimes like a modern woman, alone, as when she went into the hill country to visit Elizabeth. There were annual pilgrimages to Jerusalem for Passover festivities, shorter trips to places like Bethlehem, years spent in a foreign country, and eventually the indescribable happiness and pride of journeying all over Galilee as a disciple of her son, seeing crowds throng to him in adoration and hearing him teach and preach the kingdom of God. The multifaceted benefits of traveling—encountering new sights, witnessing the beauty of the land, meeting interesting people, and hearing new ideas—must have contributed immeasurably to the liveliness of Mary's mind and to her completeness as a person.

Throughout the centuries, great artists such as Titian, in *The Virgin of the Rabbit,* or the first painter to portray Our Lady of Guadalupe surrounded in flowers, suggest her likely closeness to nature, sparrows, lambs, and the lilies of the fields. It is not difficult to picture Mary outdoors enjoying the seashore of Galilee or resting in a cool grove of olive trees, rejoicing at the sheer magnificence of creation, or smiling, laughing, embracing people she loves, or with tears of joy in her eyes. The mother of

Jesus connected to others easily, whether to relatives such as Elizabeth, or to strangers like the servers at Cana, so let us imagine her affection as she welcomed Peter, John, and Mary Magdalene when they came to her home to study with Jesus, taking their hands in hers, inviting them to stay for supper, telling them to come again. We should picture her excitement when her beloved cousin Elizabeth and Elizabeth's husband, Zachariah, a priest known for his holiness, came for a visit with their toddler son, the future John the Baptizer. Mary and Elizabeth would be beside themselves with joy watching their adorable three-year-olds play.

BEING WITH SORROW

In a poem that expresses the pain and confusion many people feel today, the poet Dorothy Walters asks, "What Is Happening?"

> Moment to moment
> we ask, what is happening?
> The sound of shattering everywhere,
> is it the world, fragmenting at last,
> or our own hearts cracking,
> the final break-up of ice?[8]

Walters's question fits well with the radical suffering that breaks individuals and families and entire nations. Throughout the ages, epochs of suffering such as we now see all around us have generated deep veneration of Mary as *Mater Dolorosa,* Mother of Sorrows, her most popular title and role for countless millions of people who turn to her in prayer every day. Many saints have written in awe of how Mary will pour herself into a suffering person the instant she sees an opening, as though she were responding to an invitation delivered by an angel.

Many famous paintings, such as Jean Miralhet's *Mater Misericordia* and Piero della Francesca's *Madonna della Misericordia,* depict Mary in oversized form, wrapping her huge cloak around great numbers of people who come to her for shelter in times of pain. It is a magnificent image, and of course it applies to anyone who comes to her for any reason. Seeing Mary in towering form, yet with love on her face and compassion in her outstretched arms—the antithesis of all other giants in Scripture, literature, or mythology—evokes a powerful prayer that we can offer for one another in times of suffering. This prayer consists of merely imagining Mary tenderly enfolding a loved one, yourself, or other people in her great cape, and knowing that—close to her—they will receive comfort, protection, healing, peace, or whatever is needed.

Suffering often strikes randomly and forcefully. In the shock of such a moment, we may see God as so remote and uninvolved that we feel abandoned, although God does not ever, in any time or circumstance whatsoever, abandon a human being. We do, however, abandon God. At such a time, many people flee to a relationship with Mary. Her extreme experience at the side of her crucified son builds instantaneous rapport. The suffering of a mother losing her child elicits all our compassion; it is something we can relate to, an image we can hold onto for encouragement to go through our own unavoidable pain, instead of running away in denial or addiction.

Because Mary's years on earth were in many ways like our own, we can draw courage from her example of enduring the unendurable with an air of dignity that, in our hearts, we all long to emulate. Mary models not only on earth but also for all eternity what one writer calls "the human passage through deep anguish and grief into fullness of life and light."[9] Mary's fifty-day journey from the horrific last day of her son's life, through the breathless joy of the first Easter season, to the fiery beauty of the Spirit's descent on Pentecost offers people of every century reassurance that sorrow is always transfigured into joy.

BEING GRATEFUL

None of the practices in *The Way of Mary* specifically suggests praise and gratitude, but this is one of the most important aspects of Christian spiritual life, and it is implicit at every step. Remembering to say even a one-sentence prayer of praise and gratitude when you complete a step acknowledges the grace and blessings God is giving you through your spiritual work, sometimes even before they become apparent. The habit of gratitude prompts us to remember to give back to life.

The deeply inspired poet Christopher Smart wrote a magnificent affirmation of his thanks and praise for God when he was in debtors' prison, sick, filthy, and reduced to hopeless misery. His poem *Jubilate Agno* is an ecstatic outpouring of long lists of things for which he is grateful. There is Geoffrey, his cat, "the servant of the living God" who "purrs in gratefulness"; nutmeg and lightning; colors, because they are spiritual; letters of the alphabet; sunshine that "illumines the air with brightness"; God's blessed presence in shades of green; and so on, page after page. Each tender, poignant item speaks of Smart's love for the Psalms, which he called "the great book of gratitude." His poem reminds us to be grateful for *everything*, not only for the fun and rewards but also for the hurts and reversals.

A lovely time to engage in prayers of thanksgiving is dusk. It is the traditional hour for praying Vespers in monasteries and convents dating back to the Middle Ages and in many churches and homes today. While many people rise to pray at dawn when flowers are opening, birds begin chirping, and the world seems to be coming alive again, many others experience dusk as the most spiritual time of the day. The moon and stars come into view, and an air of mystical wonder hovers over the earth. It is a most fertile time to pray.

BEING FOR OTHERS

An ancient saying about the effects of wisdom goes like this: She who knows and knows she knows, she is wise, follow her (and we could also say, he who knows and knows he knows, he is wise, follow him). This saying includes central components of human wisdom, such as insight, self-understanding, and self-confidence, all of which grow and develop from performing the kind of inner work found in Part Two of *The Way of Mary*. It is awe inspiring how quickly transfiguration begins as one embarks on a spiritual path. The darkest mind can sparkle like a freshly polished window in the sun. Mary, by exhibiting the clean, crystal-like quality of a mind refined by wisdom, holds up the ideal for us to strive for, the ideal taught her by her son.

On a spiritual path, it is crucial to let go of empty secular thinking and learn to think theologically. In other words, to *think with faith and love*, to continually keep in mind the larger view of reality. While purely secular thought, such as we hear in the media, can carry useful information around the world, it cannot help us know Christ or the reason for our existence. Secular thinking is devoid of ultimate meaning because it lacks faith and love, because it is ignorant of God and has edited out of its awareness the deeper dimensions of life and love.

Marian spiritual practice can take us a long way toward the spiritual goals we are seeking, but it is not enough. Christian service, which is implicit in the very notion of love, is also essential. In order to reach our full spiritual potential, we cannot live just for ourselves. Like Mary, who lived for others, and Jesus, who died for others, we are called to serve the world's needs insofar as we can. No pilgrimage alone, no matter how effective, can fulfill our deep inner longing to give.

A rich metaphor from the Sufi poet Rumi speaks to all religious people, and especially to Christians, about the gains in spirit that come from helping others. He says:

Walk out of your house like a shepherd.[10]

It is as though he were saying to each person on a spiritual path: "You have a flock to tend. Go where your caring and tenderness lead you. And if you haven't yet found your flock, carry yourself as though you had. Be present and available to people who need you. Hold back sometimes so others may be affirmed."

WITH MARY AFTER LIFE

Because of the lifelong mysteries and epiphanies that play out like a holy symphony in the soul, most people on earth believe, as did Mary waiting for Pentecost, that neither time nor distance can ever separate those who love.

For Christians, death itself has died, leaving behind a few bones that will turn to dust in the light of the Christ, Mary's risen son. We have no idea how the afterlife will look or how it will feel, or to what extent it might resemble or differ from life as we know it, but because of Mary and Jesus, we have reliable reassurance that there is more to come.

In powerful verse that for Christians seems a glimpse of eternity, Rainer Maria Rilke wrote:

Nearing death one doesn't see death, but stares beyond, perhaps with an animal's vast gaze. Lovers, if the beloved were

not there blocking the view, are close to it, and marvel. . . . As
if by some mistake, it opens for them behind each other.[11]

This intuition of immortality lacks the certitude and
beauty of Christian faith, but it hints at the divine
undercurrent that flows through our every experience,
inviting us toward fulfillment in the afterlife of the
purpose imprinted in every atom and every cell.

Through the grace of Mary, believers know that God is
our final goal.

To imagine the vision of God in eternity or the
spiritual presence of Mary from the perspective of today
is not possible. Too much is unknowable. But Dante, in
indescribably sublime lines toward the end of the *Divine
Comedy,* insists that a traveler making the passage from earth
to eternity must behold the vision of Mary to be pure and
strong enough to behold the glory of her Son:

> Look now upon the face that most resembles Christ's,
> for only through its brightness
> can you prepare your vision to see Him.
> (*Paradiso* 32, 85–87)

Only the sight of Mary in radiance, says Dante, can
ready the pilgrim soul for the journey's ineffable end in
the blinding beauty of her Son.

PART TWO

Following Mary's Footsteps Toward God

CHAPTER 3
A Daily Pattern of Prayer

To KNOW THE LIVING FAITH AND LOVE AND BEAUTY THAT IS MARY'S, to allow her to transfigure your image of yourself and your vision of the world, to rediscover how much you can care, there is no better way than commitment to a daily spiritual practice. *Daily* of course means as daily as possible, since emergencies, illness, vacation days, and various problems can interfere. Only the angels' prayer is uninterrupted. What matters for us is to make the commitment. The poet Mary Oliver has a wonderful verse in this context:

One day you finally knew
what you had to do, and began.[12]

Once you have found your rhythm and glimpsed how wide your heart can open and how liberally Mary fills the sacred space with her grace and inspiration, you may find your spiritual work turn into an effortless activity full of joy. Buddhist spiritual teachers have a name for this comfort that comes with long-term practice: "effortless efforting."

A wide variety of meditations and prayers is included for each step in *The Way of Mary* to give you a broad and deep experience. You may wish to make your journey with Mary as a two-week retreat, praying one step a day for fourteen days, or you may prefer to take a more leisurely approach to the pilgrimage, depending on the time available. If you are pressed for time, it is best to do the brief reading from Scripture, a meditation, and a prayer.

Whether you make the two-week pilgrimage or extend it over time, you may wish to set aside additional time for the last exercise, "Freeing the Creative Spirit." While this exercise can be completed in a few minutes, it can also be enlarged into a major project. After you have finished all fourteen steps of *The Way of Mary* for the first time, there are many ways to return to it. Some people will want to repeat a specific exercise; others will dip in and out of different steps in random order. Others may want to repeat the entire pilgrimage in May, the traditional month of Mary; in Advent; in Lent; during the Paschal season; or whenever the need arises. Praying *The Way of Mary* will always bring spiritual gifts and blessings, but the season in which you make the journey will color and enrich your experience.

Before you start the steps, select a quiet place in your home where you will not be interrupted and to which you can return each day. Take a comfortable position, preferably on a straight-backed chair with your feet flat on the floor, though many other prayer postures are suitable. Turn off all electronic devices, light a candle or incense if you wish, and, if possible, keep a symbol of Mary close by.

Always make an effort to enter silence before you begin, because, as many saints have observed, nothing is closer to God than silence. Some people like to start prayer by taking three long and slow deep breaths; others enjoy a few minutes of deep breathing to let go of tension, relax, and center. Decades of scientific research and medical testing have shown that deep breathing, correctly learned, has remarkable results, such as calming nervousness and building powers of concentration. Blood pressure and respiration rates decrease, conserving vital energies; deeper brain waves that are associated with peace and health replace superficial brain waves; cardiac rhythms slow; levels of hormones associated with stress drop. Consequently, undesirable emotional states—ranging from anger, frustration, and fear at one end of the spectrum to boredom and dormant motivation at the other—also decrease.

Buddhist monks and Hindu spiritual teachers have contributed invaluably to the West's renewed quest for silence by helping to elicit interest in contemplation. They have taught several generations of Christians to sit still and concentrate. These Eastern guides have helped remind us that in silence it is possible to know oneness with God. While many of these Eastern teachers prefer words such as *emptiness* or *ultimate reality* to name the goal of spiritual attainment rather than the word *God*, the experience is the same and the results are the same. When the great Trappist monk Thomas Merton, who had practiced contemplative prayer for twenty years, met a saintly Buddhist monk who had meditated for thirty years, they found that they had learned the same things, and that neither had ever experienced perfect oneness with God. The important word here is *perfect*. The two men had encountered the Holy One frequently and deeply and had been given beautiful experiences in prayer and meditation, and at the end of the day both realized that only God can know God perfectly.

THE FIVE PARTS OF EACH STEP

The practices that accompany each step follow a pattern: Each begins with a scriptural passage called "Listening to Scripture." Then an exercise is given, based on St. Ignatius Loyola's Spiritual Exercises, called "Imagining the Story." This is followed by "Meditations" that encompass reflection questions and illuminations—uplifting quotes from sacred sources. Prayers follow. Finally, each step ends with a practice called "Freeing the Creative Spirit."

There are many pathways toward spiritual evolution, and most people choose the one that best fits their personality and temperament. Some prefer *thinking* about the great questions of the spirit; others like to *intuit* and *feel* the Spirit's presence in love; others connect to God through the sensuous beauty of nature, while others prefer the path of action. The practices in *The Way of Mary* seek to be inclusive of all these different personalities and preferences; nevertheless, certain practices may appeal to you less or more than others. Before omitting what you don't like, you may find it worthwhile to do all the practices at least once. By approaching God in ways that you have not thought of before, you open your heart to the possibility of an experience of your whole being coming into the presence of the Holy One.

1. LISTENING TO SCRIPTURE

Readings selected for *The Way of Mary* celebrate fourteen of the most important, heartwarming, and revelatory happenings in the life of the mother of Jesus. You are asked to read one of these brief passages at each step of the pilgrimage, because each beautiful story invites you into a world where you can see in a new way, where your imagination can soar. In these selections from the New Testament, symbolic words and pictures tell of universal truths, desires, and feelings, all of which you will find echoing in your own spiritual experience. Although the days have long gone by since village storytellers captivated listeners of all ages around a fire at night with the ups and downs, the excitement and surprise endings of great stories, *reading* a story can be a powerful experience. It can awaken the inner intuitive nature that sadly is in danger of being dulled by the din and blare of surround sound and the general cacophony of modern living.

The selections in this book come ultimately from the generation of people who knew Jesus, Mary, and the original disciples personally, who interacted with them at close proximity, sharing meals and possessions and financial resources as well as laughter and tears, hopes and losses, successes and failures. These people transmitted the stories orally from person to person, wide and far, and when their generation began dying out, others wrote down what they had learned for all generations to come. Painstakingly preserved over the centuries by monks' laborious hand copying, the accounts were disseminated broadly and rapidly in the sixteenth century with the invention of the printing press. Filled with hundreds of stories such as those in this book, the Bible has been ever since the best-selling book of all time.

2. IMAGINING THE STORY

In each step of *The Way of Mary*, the spiritual practices following the New Testament reading will bring the story vibrantly alive for you and help you to know Mary more fully while delving into your own spirituality. For most people, the first one, "Imagining the Story," is stimulating, enlivening, and exciting, like a trip to an exotic place where we don't speak the language and merely entering a restaurant for lunch becomes an adventure. But because this exercise is an activity of the spiritual imagination, it guides you to deeply meaningful discoveries that outlast vacation fun. Nevertheless, "imagining," even spiritual imagining, is not right for everyone, and sometimes it is best to omit it and go directly to the next exercise.

Imagining the scriptural story adapts a highly effective form of sensual-imaginative prayer that St. Ignatius Loyola created for the first generation of Jesuits, whose order he founded. In this adapted form of his Spiritual Exercises, you are invited to step back in history and become not only an eyewitness to an original event on Mary's pilgrimage, but also a participant in the experience. Guidance is given for you to eat, drink, dress, and wear your hair in ways similar to those of the women and men Mary knew, and to move about in her ancient world as though you had been born there.

There are essentially two parts to this exercise. One is to imagine all of your senses coming vibrantly alive, so you can see, hear, taste, touch, and smell the same rich sensations that reached Mary as she went about her daily life. This way, you can look at the bright beauty of the Galilean sky, hear the voices of Mary's friends, allow the enticing smell of flatbread baking over an open fire to make you ravenous, and enjoy the savor of homemade wine. You may want to pick oranges, dates, and almonds from the beautiful trees all around you or walk to the local well with Mary and her young son to hear the news drifting in from Syria on a traders' caravan. You can be with Joseph when an armed Roman soldier dismounts to deliver orders from the emperor to go to Bethlehem for a census. The possibilities are as unlimited as your willingness to release your imagination.

The second part of the exercise is to relate to and converse with the protagonists in the reading. Often the protagonist is Mary, but some people like to ask questions or dialogue with someone else in the story. How you connect with a person is up to you, although guidance is offered for expressing your thoughts and feelings. You may find yourself profoundly moved, and you may wish to simply approach one of the main players in the drama and express what is in your heart, and then listen for her or his response. You may be amazed to see how deep your conversation can go, or how inspiring your own imagined replies can be. You will meet pieces of yourself that you never knew. At the end of the exercise, you may find yourself deep in prayer.

3. MEDITATIONS

The scriptural reading for a particular step is followed by between two and four brief meditations that invite you to be actively engaged in thought and reflection. It is best to read a meditation quite slowly, pausing as often as you like at new ideas or passages you find moving, both for reflection and for further development. It is important to pay attention to your insights, as there is much to be learned from them, and to allow feelings to surface, as they contain powerfully enlivening energies.

The poet Denise Levertov raised an important spiritual and human problem through a shining metaphor:

How can I focus my flickering, perceive
At the fountain's heart
The sapphire I know is there?

For believers, the best possible answer to Levertov's question, the best way to learn to concentrate, is through prayer.

3A. REFLECTION QUESTIONS

After each meditation, optional questions invite you to interrelate with the contents of the meditation to further evoke your individual possibilities, simply and comfortably. The questions do not intend to challenge you; you're not in school. There is no right answer anywhere in this book, only suggestions to help you open the inner doorway to a wisdom that will remain with you for the rest of your life, on the best days and on the most difficult ones. It is really the spiritual intellect that these questions elicit (for more about this, see the topic "Freeing the Spiritual Intellect" in chapter 2).

Many people reply to the questions silently, while others like to journal their responses. For this, a notepad and pen will suffice, but a computer is fine, too, if that is what you prefer. I enjoy journaling in something tangible and attractive, like a lightly bound notebook that I can hold in my hand, with a cover that is pleasant to touch and look at, a tactile reminder of the content's sacredness.

The purpose of the reflection questions is to receive the most one can from the scriptural reading and meditations—not merely information, which is forced at us from all directions today, but the kind of learning that leads to wisdom. A number of the questions evoke self-understanding, since, as St. Augustine wrote repeatedly, knowing oneself is the truest way to knowing God. Other questions hope to stimulate your quest for worthwhile knowledge. Remain relaxed as you read these questions, and allow them to lead you joyfully to new thoughts, insights, and, perhaps most important, more questions. Let your curiosity be aroused. Reach for new knowledge. Learn something entirely new.

You may wish to use the journal for reflection on other matters during the days that you are traveling with Mary. This is particularly pertinent if you adhere to the two-week schedule of praying one step of *The Way of Mary* each day, since the greater intensity of compact pilgrimage generates enhanced spiritual awareness. On the extended schedule, however, and also if you read this book on any other basis, there will be considerable material to reflect on in your journal, such as surprising events and conversations. You are likely to have numinous dreams, which are a wonderful source of the unexpected workings of the Spirit. I have had many dreams about Mary and always approach them through questions suggested by the psychoanalyst C.G. Jung: What is the purpose of the dream? What is it trying to teach me? What do I need to learn at this time? These and similar questions may be asked, of course, about any event in our experience.

During a day when you are working with *The Way of Mary*, it is likely that some or much of your experience will be connected to the powerful archetypes associated with her. So you may wish to think about events in relationship to the scriptural reading with which you are engaged at the moment. You might respond to a question such as this one: "What have I learned from Mary that can help me understand this situation (or event, person, problem, hurt, and so on)?" Or, if you need to make a decision, you could look to Mary for guidance. Little by little, you will find your own best way to learn from the Mother of God.

Keeping a journal provides a lasting record of one's spiritual growth, no matter how clear or tortuous and convoluted it may be. It will provide a much more accurate record than your memory. Rereading the journal to review the course of your pilgrimage greatly enhances awareness of what *really* happened, helping you to avoid denial and blame and to overcome our almost inevitable and recurrent resistance to change. A journal becomes a prominent part of your spiritual autobiography, a treasure to consult over and over again as the months and years go by.

3B. ILLUMINATIONS

In this book, *illumination* means brightening your soul to bring light to the world. To aim at these goals, the reflection questions are followed by a few inspirational messages from Scripture, saints, poets, and spiritual leaders, Christian and non-Christian. Of illuminations from non-Christian sources, only ones that are compatible with Christian faith have been chosen, and these are usually from the more mystical religious traditions, such as Hinduism and Sufism, the spiritual wing of Islam.

The contents of these quotes, which suggest the principal theme of a step without adhering to it rigidly, seek to kindle intuition—our brightest, most light-giving gift—and feelings of the most refined kind. Such feelings include love (always an outcome of prayer), devotion, awe, and reverence.

In contrast to other practices in *The Way of Mary* that aspire to be thought provoking or to fire the imagination, the illuminations work by awakening the heart. Today, in the age of instant messaging and social networking services, there is little practical need to memorize, but learning some of these illuminations by heart gives you beautiful, uplifting words that can totally transform the quality of a day. Store in your heart messages of comfort, inspiration, or strength, and they will be there for you during moments of stress, unpleasantness, depression, or waiting. Think of John O'Donohue's remark in *Anam Cara*:

> May evening find you gracious and fulfilled.[13]

Learn that by heart, and you can instantly turn anxiety into peace, your own or another person's.

Elders reap a special harvest from this practice, since memorizing combats memory loss by creating new neural pathways. And children can be given a sense of reverence and helped to forge character by taking spiritual messages into their hearts. For people in between the two extremes of age, memorizing puts time to gracious use.

4. PRAYERS

After the illuminations, you will find two or three Marian prayers, well known for the most part, that echo and expand on a step's themes with the deepening power and beauty that only prayer can provide. Each prayer has been carefully chosen for its ability to make a strong impression that will strengthen your relationship with Mary in a loving, lasting way and affect the way you live your daily life. As the California spiritual teacher Eknath Easwaran wrote about great prayers and meditations:

> [W]ords like these paint a picture we can keep our eyes on throughout the choices of the day.[14]

Just as we unconsciously read a prayer more reverently than a poem or other writings, so we read it with a different attitude and intention, knowing that we are being heard. You will find five kinds of prayers in *The Way of Mary* (although some traditions would see two or three). There are prayers of *petition* (asking God for something); *repentance* (expressing sorrow for sin and asking for forgiveness); *intercession* (praying for others); *gratitude* (thanking God); and *praise* (glorifying God).

Prayers of petition in this book do not ask for something concrete that one wants, the way a child prays; they imply a subtle intention that is more like giving your consent to God's action within yourself or in the world. When you do that, your spiritual possibilities reach new dimensions. Just by entering willingly into a trusting relationship with God, we are opening ourselves to the blessing we seek, and there will be no end to the grace available for growth.

St. Paul wrote to the Romans (in 12:2):

> [B]e transformed by the renewal of your mind.

He is speaking about the Christian consecrated life, which is Mary's way and can be ours.

5. FREEING THE CREATIVE SPIRIT

The desire and ability to create comprise one of the most important aspects of our existence. By creating, we become a little like God in the original act of creation as described in Genesis 1:1–2:4a. Our capacity, and even more so our desire to create, transcend all kinds of determinism, conditioning, rote programming, or cause-and-effect scenarios. When we create, we pray, and this is a most sacred way to consciously connect with the Source of life, to participate in the holiness of God.

The creative process has the power to awaken or re-awaken our dormant spirituality. The artist in each of us can come alive and can soar in spirit through the simplest act of making something original, in part because of the self-forgetfulness implicit in much of the process. It is essentially human to reach for the divine through creativity. Our spirit longs to be one with the Spirit of God.

Human history abounds in examples of creativity to which we can look to see and feel the soaring creative spirit and free our own. Think of the caves of Lascaux in France: bison, horses, and deer stampeding across walls and ceilings, painted again and again as far back as seventeen thousand years ago.

Listen to Beethoven's majestic *Ninth Symphony*. Or float on the beauty of Fra Angelico's *Annunciation*. Few of us create at that level of perfection, but it is enough to just create.

Another aspect of the spirituality of creativity lies in the meaning, direction, and fulfillment that a creative project gives you, the creator, at each stage of bringing something new into existence. Like the drama of the little seed that germinates underground and suddenly bursts into light, grows, and blossoms into a beautiful flower, a creative effort serves as a way for the spirit to enter life and work marvels. Each step, each stage of the creative process is a gift of grace and a source of grace. You start with the initial, luminous, and elating "aha" experience that gives birth to a new image, a new idea. You go through the excitement of planning; then the laborious process of execution. And you arrive at completion, at the final creation of something that has never been before. You have cooperated with grace, and as St. Hildegard said, you are a co-creator with God.

The artistic quality, monetary value, perceived beauty, or overall merit of what you create is of course entirely irrelevant. Being yourself and making something out of your soul's core is what counts. You don't have to make a sculptured or musical masterpiece. A delicious (or simply a comfort-inducing) meal cooked for a loved one or for the needy qualifies equally; so does a knitted hat or a crèche built out of scraps of leftover wood and cardboard for your grandson. All created objects have equal spiritual worth. The spiritual value has to do first with honoring your favorite method of creative expression and then taking the leap into the act of making something new, giving birth to something that has never existed before. There is no need to be a good writer to create a prayer. All of us can do that.

If it sometimes seems there is nothing new under the sun, draw up a menu for an elaborate dinner. It will be unique and completely your own.

Be sure to save the prayers, drawings, photographs, collages, songs, and other products of your creativity as you follow the steps. You will want to look back at them to review your growth as you proceed day by day with Mary.

The Annunciation

Mary Is Invited to Become the Mother of Jesus
(Luke 1:26–38)

LISTENING TO SCRIPTURE

In the sixth month the angel Gabriel was sent from God to a city of Galilee named Nazareth, to a virgin betrothed to a man whose name was Joseph, of the house of David; and the virgin's name was Mary. And he came to her and said, "Hail, O favored one, the Lord is with you!" But she was greatly troubled at the saying, and considered in her mind what sort of greeting this might be. And the angel said to her, "Do not be afraid, Mary, for you have found favor with God. And behold, you will conceive in your womb and bear a son, and you shall call his name Jesus.

"He will be great, and will be called the Son of the Most High;
and the Lord God will give to him the throne of his father
        David,
and he will reign over the house of Jacob forever;
and of his kingdom there will be no end."

And Mary said to the angel, "How shall this be, since I have no husband?"

And the angel said to her,

        "The Holy Spirit will come upon you,
        and the power of the Most High will overshadow you;

> *therefore the child to be born will be called holy,*
> *the son of God.*

And behold, your kinswoman Elizabeth in her old age has also conceived a son; and this is the sixth month for her who was called barren. For with God nothing will be impossible." And Mary said, "Behold I am the handmaid of the Lord; let it be to me according to your word." And the angel departed from her. (Luke 1:26–38)

IMAGINING THE STORY

It is March 25, within a few years of the year we call 1, and a 14-year-old named Mary—Myriam in Hebrew—goes out to graze a small flock of goats on a rocky hillside in Galilee. A typical Jewish girl of her time, she wears a straight sun-bleached dress, is deeply tanned, and has dark brown hair woven into a braid that swings across her back as she runs happily up the hill. She is thinking about Joseph, a local woodworker to whom she is engaged.

Mary is as ordinary as her name and expectations. Marriage and motherhood lie ahead, and the hard life of the very poor. After the ceremony she will wear a long veil and move to a shabby one-room house just like her parents', made of stone with an earthen floor and high-placed air vents admitting a bit of light. Like her ancestors for many centuries, Mary will cook over an open fire, sit on the ground to eat, and sleep on a thin mat. Her mother and grandmother have trained her well in women's ways of nurturing a family, tending to the sick and dying with home-grown herbal medicines, and helping in childbirth.

Picture Mary in your imagination as she finds a patch of dusty land with just enough grass to feed her small flock for the day. Already thirsty, she takes a small drink of water from her wineskin when something alarming happens, something too amazing to be real, and she is shaken to her core. An angel has appeared right in front of her. Imagine yourself in her place. What would you be feeling and thinking?

Mary is afraid, but the angel is beautiful, and he speaks to her in a soothing, tender voice. Quickly, she calms herself. The message is curious, inappropriate, as though it were meant for someone else, and she struggles with herself before she speaks. What is it like for you to be there with Mary, listening to her conversation with Gabriel? If you could speak to Mary, what would you say? What would she reply? Continue your conversation with her if you wish.

What did you learn from your conversation with Mary?

MEDITATIONS

Mary is terrified, almost frozen in place, when she is asked to make the hardest decision of her life, one that will turn her in a direction she never dreamed of taking. But the women in her family have trained her to stand firm and face life's hardest realities directly and courageously. So she does not run away. Instead, she stands still and poised, like a much older woman, with traces in her huge, dark eyes of the strong feminine presence she will acquire over time. Wide awake and focused, a natural contemplative, Mary remains absolutely silent as she mulls over the strange, unfitting, almost unbelievable words she has just heard. Why should she of all possible women be asked to become the mother of the Lord? Her mind replays family messages about doing God's will, and psalms her mother and grandmother have sung all her life flash into her mind and circle around like whirlwinds. She knows that her ancestors faced great challenges like this, sometimes saying yes to God and sometimes saying no.

One of the teachings for us in Step 1 of Mary's pilgrimage has to do with the myth of easy submission to God's will. Aligning oneself with the holy purposes at the origin and ground of the universe demands far more love, courage, and mindful willingness than simple acquiescence. God does not do violence to human integrity. The angel, the messenger, the holy flash of light that appears to Mary presents her with a dramatic, life-shattering choice, but there is no obligation to accept. Perhaps a young woman in another part of the world has already refused to become the mother of God. Perhaps, as we sometimes do, Mary could allow something sacred and beautiful to slip away like a feather in a breeze.

But she is totally free of passivity, immaculately free of the ways we silence and stifle and sabotage our own souls. Blessed as she is, Mary is always wide awake. It is as though a gentle hand had shaken her on the shoulder at the dawn of her life to remind her there is much to do. So, brightly and lovingly, she engages the divine powers with all the energies and wisdom in her young soul.

⨳

Mary's way of decision making is one that we can follow. First, she postpones the choice to give herself time to gather more information, weigh alternatives, and pray. She turns the tables on the angelic messenger by *questioning him*. The crucial question is, How? How can she become pregnant without Joseph? How does the Holy Spirit overshadow one? How can something biologically impossible take place? And, most serious of all, how can one willingly undertake such a radical responsibility as motherhood when one feels completely unprepared?

Mary's reflection processes must have brought her close to saying no before the decisive intuition that led her to say yes. Some piece of herself must have protested: This is not what I want to do with my life right now. I do not want to be different; I want to belong. Nor will I risk losing my fiancé or allowing society to punish me for being an unmarried mother. What God is asking is too difficult. I will remain on the path I have carved out for myself and refuse to let God's plans disturb my own.

⨳

Some of us, when we want to reject a divine initiative, become contentious, like Job. Others hammer and beat on *the cloud of unknowing*, like the author of that beautiful book, trying to get God's attention in all the wrong ways. Still others never pause to look for God's purposes. But Mary, who lives in the presence of the Holy One, converses with God like a lover. She believes what the Beloved says and knows in her heart that his promises will come true.

Negative thinking comes to an end when we allow intuition to accomplish its sacred work. A vision of a much wider scheme of things than our own comes into view, as though the sun has risen in a second, revealing a blazing jewel box of luminous reds, violets, and oranges, and Mary realizes that she is not being torn apart, but invited to a feast. As in our own lives, what terrifies at one minute is transmuted in the next into bliss.

Mary turns to the divine messenger as though she were speaking directly to God and, without a shadow of reluctance speaks words that have resounded down the halls of history and will be echoed until the end of time: *"Let it be."*

With this deeply felt expression of free and loving consent, Mary, the mother-to-be of Jesus, pronounces herself a servant of the living God who will do joyfully what she has been asked to do. A line from a prayer of the Russian poet Kadya Molodowsky (1894–1975) makes one think of Mary in this moment, even though the poet addresses her petition to God:

> Sow in me your living breath
> As you sow a seed in the earth.[15]

Step 1, a powerful opening day of our pilgrimage with Mary, accents the monumental import of the invitation extended to her. Nothing that glorious need happen again. But we, too, receive annunciations. Sacred messages come to us regularly from the Holy One. An angel of annunciation may be trying to reach us today with wonderful news: An idea for helping a friend to heal, an insight that puts the thousandth piece of a harrowing puzzle into place, or an entire bundle of positive attitudes that rearrange your whole character. Watch and listen. Do not go back to sleep. Something amazing may be happening.

REFLECTION QUESTIONS

- What have the readings today on the Annunciation revealed to you about Mary? Do you see her as someone who chose the way she wanted to live her life? Could you be more proactive about choosing the way you want to live your life? Are there decisions you need to make about the way you use your time?
- When did you recently choose to say yes to God? When do you wish you had? Is there an area of your life where it would be wise to let go?
- Have today's readings revealed something to you about yourself? Mention an annunciation experience of your own. Did it enrich someone's life? Has it ever occurred to you when something awakens you in the night that it might be an angel of annunciation?

- One of the many teachings in the Annunciation story is "With God, nothing is impossible." Does that mean that everything is possible for us, or is it a statement about God's power?
- If you have been called to the awe-inspiring responsibility of parenting a child, how do you bring God into your nurturing?

ILLUMINATIONS

Today the whole circle of the earth is filled with joy.[16]
—*St. Gregory Thaumaturgos, "the wonder-worker,"*
   bishop in Asia Minor (ca. 213–ca. 270)

I have called you by name. You are mine, and I love you.
—*Isaiah 43:1–2*

I don't know Who or What put the question; I don't even know when it was put. I don't even remember answering. But at some moment I did answer Yes to Someone (or Something) and from that hour I was certain that existence is meaningful and that, therefore, my life, in self-surrender, has a goal.[17]
   —*Dag Hammarskjöld, twentieth-century Swedish diplomat*

Blessed is she who believed that the promise made her by the Lord would be fulfilled.

—*Luke 1:45*

I see you in a thousand paintings,
Mary, so tenderly depicted.
Yet none of them can begin to show you
As my soul sees you.

I only know that suddenly all chaos
has vanished like a dream,
and a heaven of ineffable sweetness
has opened forever in my soul.[18]
—*Novalis (Friedrich von Hardenberg), German poet*
  (1772–1801)

PRAYERS

Hail Mary!
Full of grace.
The Lord is with you.
Blessed are you among women,
and blessed is the fruit of your womb, Jesus.
Holy Mary, mother of God,
pray for us sinners
now and at the hour of our death.
Amen.
—*Traditional prayer dating to the seventh century*

Accept, O Lord, all my freedom.

Accept my memory, my mind, and all my will.

Whatever I am or possess,

you have graciously given me;

I give it all back to you,

to be completely governed by your will.

Give me only your love and your grace

and I am rich enough,

and I ask nothing more.[19]

—*St. Ignatius Loyola, founder of*
the Society of Jesus (the Jesuits), 1491–1556

How wonderful is your love!

You looked at your fairest daughter

as an eagle focuses its eye upon the sun;

You, the eternal Father, saw

her radiance,

and the Word became flesh in her.[20]

—*St. Hildegard of Bingen,*
German visionary theologian (1098–1179)

Mary,

if I were Queen of Heaven,

and you were Thérèse,

I would pray to be Thérèse

so you could be Queen of Heaven.

—*St. Thérèse of Lisieux, French mystic (1873–1897)*

FREEING THE CREATIVE SPIRIT[21]

Create a Mary altar in your home. It can be as simple as a statue or another image of Mary placed on a table where you pray, or it can be as large and elaborate as you wish. If there was an altar to Mary in your home when you were growing up, it may have consisted of a small statue of Mary in blue and white porcelain centered on a white linen cloth, where occasionally a bud vase holding a rose appeared. Although devout mothers had been placing such altars in the rooms of newborn daughters for centuries, the custom faded after the Vatican Council of the 1960s and seemed to be dying out. But today it is returning, and in far more creative forms. Allow your imagination to soar while you create your altar.

Look around your home for items to include, such as a candle, flower vase, incense, water, oil, beads, a photograph, a plant, a symbol of Mary, whatever feels right to you. Go through drawers, closets, storage chests, and boxes for things you may have forgotten about. Religious bookstores sometimes offer inexpensive items that might be meaningful on your altar. Be sure to look outdoors for appropriate items in your immediate surroundings, in a local park or woods or at a beach, wherever you have access to nature, in as many locations as possible, especially if you have the opportunity to travel. Without disturbing the ecology, you will be able to bring home such beautiful objects as a few berries, pinecones, twigs, or shells, or perhaps a small piece of driftwood or peeled-off bark, an abandoned bird's nest, a round white stone, or other smooth stones and pebbles that feel pleasant in your hands.

Some people make an altar cloth from meaningful pieces of material, such as a handkerchief, shawl, or scrap of cloth belonging to a loved one (living or deceased). A particularly lovely altar I once saw began with a fringed, gray silk shawl that had been worn by a beloved aunt of the woman making the altar. It made a perfect altar cloth.

THE VISIT TO ELIZABETH

Mary Visits Her Cousin Elizabeth While
Both Women Are Waiting to Give Birth
(Luke 1:26–38)

LISTENING TO SCRIPTURE

Mary rose and went with haste into the hill country, to a city of Judah, and she entered the house of Zechariah and greeted Elizabeth. And when Elizabeth heard the greeting of Mary, the baby leaped in her womb; and Elizabeth was filled with the Holy Spirit, and she exclaimed with a loud cry, "Blessed are you among women, and blessed is the fruit of your womb! And why is this granted to me, that the mother of my Lord should come to me? For behold, when the voice of your greeting came to my ears, the [baby] in my womb leaped for joy. And blessed is she who believed that there would be a fulfillment of what was spoken to her from the Lord." . . . And Mary remained with her about three months, and returned to her home. (Luke 1:39–45, 56)

IMAGINING THE STORY

The joy of Gabriel's message has barely subsided when Mary finds herself in a critical situation: She is pregnant and unmarried in an era when patriarchal laws make a woman in this situation an object of shame and shunning, possibly of death threats. Even Joseph, her fiancé, wants nothing more to do with her (Matthew 1:19). Isolated from everyone except God, she flees Nazareth in the hope of finding support and understanding from the one person she thinks will be compassionate, her cousin Elizabeth, an older woman who has the maturity to understand. So Mary rushes alone into the hill country where skirmishes between bandits and Roman soldiers are common and dangerous for innocent passers-by. But she is oblivious to the danger, and indifferent to the misery of walking in thin sandals over fifty miles of burning roads in the heat of May.

Can you imagine what this journey is like for her? Do you picture her feeling ill from morning sickness or other discomforts that may come in the first trimester of pregnancy? If you were in her place, what would you be thinking? Would you be worrying about a woman's poor chance of surviving childbirth in the first century? Or, would you be wondering who will help with the delivery? Or how hard it is for a single woman to support a child, both then and now? Or, would your faith override the doubts and questions so you could reflect joyously on the amazing event of encountering an angel and being invited to a wondrous role in history?

In your imagination, place yourself with Mary as her hurried pilgrimage ends safely on May 31 of the year we name "1." Picture yourself on the step leading to the broad doorway of her cousin's home. Elizabeth's husband is a priest renowned for his holiness. What kind of a house would you imagine suitable for the priestly aristocracy? What details do you observe—size, color, building materials, number of rooms? What else? Are the grounds planted? What trees, herbs, flowers, stones, animals, buildings, and people do you notice?

Watch as Elizabeth runs to greet her beloved cousin and welcomes her so jubilantly that Elizabeth's baby kicks for joy. Awed and overjoyed, she speaks prophetic words to Mary that will be repeated until the end of time: "Blessed are you among women, and blessed is the fruit of your womb." What would you feel at this great moment? Elizabeth reveals herself to be a prophet. Imagine yourself speaking to Elizabeth. What would you say? How would she respond?

MEDITATIONS

One of the most beautiful qualities in Mary's life and in the human soul is faith. Mary trusts in the ancient revelations and promises in her people's sacred Scriptures, and those beliefs set fire to her spirit and fill her soul with love. They transfigure her whole outlook on life. All life is holy, but only faith can see and feel the holiness. Even though Mary goes through massive tests and trials that would challenge anyone's beliefs, she does not discard her precious ancestral heritage; instead, she cherishes and clings to her faith as though it were the fire lighting the sun and the moon and the stars.

Mary flees to Elizabeth because of the bitter social rejection she would suffer at home in Nazareth as an unmarried woman expecting a child. Yet she arrives at her cousin's with her integrity and conscience and self-worth intact. Elizabeth has been prophetically prepared for the visit of her young cousin, the future mother of God, the *Theotokos,* and greets her in a rapturous voice, eloquently praising Mary not only once but three times for being "blessed." Whether you understand this beautiful word *blessed* to mean favored by God, sanctified, beloved, or happy, it describes Mary perfectly in her newly consecrated life. She, "alone of all her sex," as Caelius Sedulius famously described her in the fifth century, will play a role in the redemption of humankind, which is massively guilty for wars and violence and atrocities that at times appear irredeemable. She is additionally blessed because the tiny child in her swelling uterus will bequeath to the world the highest and most sublime religion of love ever known. On the same level of blessing and sacred significance, Elizabeth the prophet places her cousin's *faith.*

An implicit teaching for us on Step 2 of *The Way of Mary* has to do with the sacredness of women's intimacy. Let us return to the doorway where Mary and Elizabeth take such great delight in greeting one another. While Elizabeth virtually sings her exalted welcome to Mary, the praising sounds of trumpets, harps, cymbals, and tambourines seem to fill the air. It is as though David had returned from the other world to conduct the temple symphony in praise of Mary, the Messiah's mother-to-be.

But Elizabeth has news of her own to share, amazing news. After a lifetime of longing for a child without conceiving, she, too, has received the gift of an unexpected pregnancy. Now nearly in her third trimester, blissfully happy in spite of discomforts essential to bearing a child—the back pain, sleeplessness, unbalancing heaviness—she continually thanks God for *everything.* Now Mary will be there for her when she gives birth to John, whose holy voice will resound in the wilderness preparing the way for Mary's son. Neither cousin could bear to know that one son will be beheaded, and the other crucified.

For Mary and Elizabeth to be together at such a sacred time is like a miracle, and their relationship is profound. Although one cousin is almost too young for such a tremendous destiny, the other has reached the end of her childbearing years. Yet two hearts beat inside each of them. The coincidence makes them laugh and sing like children and bond in the easy, happy, instantaneous way of women across time.

Mary and Elizabeth have been brought together providentially at the summit of women's mysteries, precisely when they need each other as never before. The dimension of waiting together to give birth lifts their genetic relationship and friendship to the level of spiritual community. As saints and poets have often remarked,

A friend is a guardian of the soul.[22]

There is no better exemplar of such sacred friendship than that of Mary and Elizabeth. The priceless support they can offer one another spiritually and emotionally leads Mary to stay with her cousin for the last three months of the older woman's pregnancy; Mary will be at her side to comfort her during labor and to help Elizabeth through the blessed ordeal of delivering a child.

The New Testament does not tell us if Mary ever lost her faith, but it is unlikely. Her first crisis passed without causing her to doubt. She placed her trust in the God of her heart, and things could not possibly have worked out more joyfully. It could be that later suffering led her to question her faith and wonder, as we do, how God can permit such extreme human pain. Since Mary questioned and took time for soul-searching, trying to understand what was happening, it is possible that she experienced doubt. We do not know. But one thing is certain: she was and is a woman of faith, a believer who learns through the Scriptures and through experience to accept the ultimate inscrutability of God's ways, while treasuring and clinging to the gift of faith. This is her ultimate teaching for us on Step 2 of *The Way of Mary*.

REFLECTION QUESTIONS

- When Mary was in a crisis, she left home for three months to be with her cousin Elizabeth. How do you decide which way to go, which door to open or which road to follow? Do you turn to your faith when you feel stuck, or trapped, or lost? Do you pray for clarity when you are not sure where you are going? Have you ever prayed to Mary in situations like these?

- Elizabeth calls Mary "blessed" three times, recognizing her as the mother of God, the *Theotokos*. How do you understand the meaning of the word "blessed" when you think of Mary? Do you think of yourself as blessed?

- The third time that Elizabeth calls Mary "blessed," it is because of Mary's faith. Elizabeth knows in the Spirit that her young cousin believes in the fulfillment of God's promises. Where do you see God's promises being fulfilled in your own life? Have there been occasions when you have clearly seen that "all things work together for good for those who love God"?

- If you do not already have a relationship with Mary, would you like to begin by entering into a dialogue with her? Is there an area where you would like to ask her for help, grace, guidance, or intercession?

- If you are a woman, when did you experience the intimacy and beauty of women's bonding? Was it a sacred experience for you? If you are a man, what example can you give of men's bonding? How do you think men's bonding differs from women's? If you are a parent, describe the moment or process of bonding with your child.

ILLUMINATIONS

If you meet the virgin on the road,
Invite her into your house.
She bears the word of God.
—*St. John of the Cross, sixteenth-century mystic*

The Lord himself will give you a sign. Look, the young woman is with child and shall bear a son, and shall name him Immanuel.
—*Isaiah 7:14*

All things are possible to one who believes.
—*Mark 9:23b*

Lord, I believe; help my unbelief.
—*Mark 9:24b*

PRAYERS

Mother of the Redeemer, with great joy we call you blessed.
—*Pope John Paul II (served 1978–2005)*

We greet you, holy Queen,

our life, our joy, and our hope,

Mother full of mercy, we cry to you in trust,

Exiled children of fallen Eve,

see our sighs and tears,

see our world of sadness.

Mother, plead for us.

Turn then towards us those eyes that plead our cause,

and when our life on earth is done,

show us then your Son,

blessed fruit of your virgin womb,

Jesus Christ our God.

O Mary, full of kindness,

O Mary, full of love,

O joyful Mary, full of peace and grace.

—*A new* Salve Regina, *Mount St. Bernard's Abbey*

Hail holy lady, most holy queen, Mary mother of God, chosen by the most holy Father in heaven, consecrated by God with his most holy and beloved Son and the Holy Spirit the comforter. The fullness of grace and goodness descended on you and remains in you.

—*St. Francis of Assisi, beloved founder of the Franciscans*
   (ca. 1182–1226)

FREEING THE CREATIVE SPIRIT

Create your own "Mary mantra" or special phrase. This is a sacred phrase directed to Mary, composed of one to ten words, that you repeat reverently as often as you can for as many minutes as you wish. Recite the mantra when you need to draw closer to Mary, or want to enter into a relationship with her, or to empty your mind of worries and problems. Waiting in line is a good time to pray the mantra, as is any occasion that generates impatience. And when you become aware that fear, frustration, or any other negative emotion is mounting inside you (or in the people near you), repeating your mantra will help still your mind. Similarly, when the environment is chaotic and it is hard to concentrate, praying your sacred phrase repetitively will help you to focus. In the East, spiritual teachers sometimes advise retreatants to sit under a tree for an hour continually repeating their mantra, in order to still their minds and center themselves in God.

Examples of a Mary mantra include "Mary, Mother of God, be with me," "Holy Mary, full of grace, hear my prayer," and the opening words of the Hail Mary: "Hail Mary, full of grace." You could adopt Pope John Paul II's beautiful one-line prayer (which appears above), "Mother of God, with great joy I call you blessed," or adapt it to your own intentions and needs. Another of this pope's beloved prayers to Mary is ideal for use as a mantra: his two-word motto, "All yours." Another alternative is to simply and prayerfully repeat the name *Mary*. But it is best to create your own unique mantra without too much comparison to other people's prayers.

THE MAGNIFICAT

Mary Sings Her Great Song of Praise,
"My Soul Magnifies the Lord
and My Spirit Rejoices in God My Savior"
(Luke 1:46–55)

LISTENING TO SCRIPTURE

And Mary said:
My soul magnifies the Lord,
and my spirit rejoices in God my Savior,
for he has regarded the low estate of his handmaiden.
For behold, henceforward all generations shall call me blessed;
for he who is mighty has done great things for me,
and holy is his name.
And his mercy is on those who fear him
from generation to generation.
He has shown strength with his arm,
he has scattered the proud in the imagination of their hearts,
he has put down the mighty from their thrones,
and exalted those of low degree;
he has filled the hungry with good things
and the rich he has sent empty away.
He has helped his servant Israel,
in remembrance of his mercy,

as he spoke to our fathers,
to Abraham and to his posterity forever. (Luke 1:46–55)

IMAGINING THE STORY

Picture yourself standing beside Elizabeth on the hot afternoon when Mary comes into sight after her long journey. How does Mary look? Does she resemble any paintings of her that you have seen? Does she appear anxious that Elizabeth will reject her for being pregnant and unmarried? Now look at Elizabeth as she smiles and laughs and runs to embrace her tired young cousin. As she holds Mary, Elizabeth rejoices in Mary's deep identity and great calling, which has been revealed to no one but Mary and herself. How does Mary's expression change with this loving welcome? Does her body language reveal relief? If you were in Mary's place, what would you be feeling?

Picture Mary relaxing into Elizabeth's warm embrace, then looking into her eyes. Unlike many of her friends, she has never thought of herself as an insignificant female destined for poverty and little else; she never accepted the saying that nothing good can come from Nazareth. But neither could she conceive of herself as a woman called to greatness. Now, however, in the mirror of the older woman's eyes, her self-image shifts dramatically. Seeing herself from Elizabeth's perspective—feeling *recognized,* feeling *known*—Mary sees herself as she really is.

Mary responds to Elizabeth's elated greeting with her own outburst of joy. In your imagination, watch and listen carefully as Mary almost sings the exquisite words of the song we name the Magnificat. What would it be like for you to hear this magnificent prayer spoken for the first time in history? Can you appreciate the magnitude of the occasion? How do you imagine Mary's voice? Is it beautiful? Is it high and lyrical? Is it soft and low? Or is it somehow different from any of these descriptions? When she finishes, what would you like to say to her? What does she say to you? If you wish, imagine yourself continuing the conversation with her.

MEDITATIONS

While Elizabeth's beautiful greeting to Mary is celebrated in Step 2, Mary's exultant response to her, the incomparably lovely Magnificat, is reserved for Step 3. Mary pours her whole heart and soul into this song of praise and thanksgiving for the great things God has done for her, echoing the ancient song of Hannah (1 Samuel 2:1–10). She speaks out not only to her cousin but also to the whole world, so that all can hear how her spirit rejoices in God her Savior, how her whole soul delights in the will of God, how she believes with her whole heart in the coming of the longed-for kingdom of God. Each person who hears these exquisite words and comes into the living presence of Mary feels something healed in her or his soul, or finds the heart throwing open its doors to include more of the world.

Mary and Elizabeth's intimate encounter transports them into a sacred space where their feelings soar to the heights, and they can share with each other the thrill and wonder and miracle of a human life growing in a woman's body. The two women allow their hearts to overflow and their jubilant spirits to reach prophetic heights. What they say to one another has been preserved in writing for all generations to come, side by side with the greatest prophetic speeches in Scripture, and standing out in women's literature of all times.

With the poorest of the poor in every era, Mary is no more than one of the small of the earth, invisible to the rich and powerful, yet her soul "magnifies" God: she makes the Word of God more audible, divine actions more visible, and holiness more realizable for each of us. Mary increases and enlarges the presence and work of God not only on earth and throughout the universe, but also in heaven.

Radiant in the holiness and hopefulness of youth, the young mother-to-be of Jesus envisions society turned upside down—despots dethroned and the poor lifted up, abusers of power ruined and the weak given strength. In the imagination of Mary's heart, the whole world has already been transfigured by her son. It is as though all stigmas have been erased, and the ignominy of poverty has been transferred to the most corrupt, so that humankind can begin again in humility, the moist and fertile ground of life's real joys.

One of the loveliest aspects of Mary's great prayer of praise appears in the humility she sings about and exemplifies.

Her humility allows light to pour into her soul even as she describes her own blessedness and liberation from a lowly social state, since her blessedness is ultimately all God's doing, the work of the God who called her into life, with whom she cooperates so graciously. Who better than she could sing about herself without egotism or arrogance, since she knows that the great things being accomplished in her life are all from and in and through God's love? What better illustration of transcendence than a statement such as hers, devoid of pride, free of the human need to inflate oneself? *He who is mighty has done great things for me, and holy is his name.*

Saint Bernard of Clairvaux (1090–1153), one of the church's greatest monastic leaders and theologians, who wrote the incomparably beautiful treatise *On Loving God* and wrote eloquently about Mary, strove all his long life for humility like hers. Because of this humility and his indifference to material things, having left his wealthy family to embrace radical poverty at the monastery of Cîteaux, he once underwent a painful experience reminiscent of issues raised in the Magnificat. Much in demand as a preacher, the saint traveled frequently to neighboring churches to give the sermon. On one occasion, he was bitterly criticized for riding a donkey that was luxuriously caparisoned in red velvet with silk tassels and sterling silver bells. Bernard looked at the animal's ostentatious garb, and then, with his head bowed in shame, replied to his accusers that he was deeply sorry, but he had never noticed what he was riding on.

REFLECTION QUESTIONS

- Seeing oneself reflected in another person's eyes with love, respect, and appreciation is a key to healthy human development and spiritual growth. When did you see yourself mirrored this way in another person's eyes? When did you serve as the mirror for someone else?

- When have you been greeted with joy and affection like Elizabeth welcomed Mary? Was the other person a parent, grandparent, child, grandchild, or other relative? Who else has welcomed you that way? Who in your life today greets you similarly? Are you aware of people who take delight in your presence?

- Whom have you greeted with joy and affection? Whom do you welcome similarly today?

- Have you observed how some people look you in the eyes but see only themselves? How could you help such a person's soul heal?

- Did you notice that when Elizabeth praised Mary, Mary responded by praising God? What does that say to you about Mary?

- Do you think of Mary as a prophet?

- The culture in which Mary and Elizabeth lived, like many cultures today, deprived women of rights and suppressed the female voice. Often when this happens, women educate one another in the privacy of the home and draw strength from one another. In what ways do you think Mary and Elizabeth nurtured, taught, strengthened, or in general helped one another during their three months together?

- When Elizabeth recovered from childbirth, Mary set out for home, evidently prepared to face Joseph's legal annulment of their betrothal and fend for herself as a despised, unmarried pregnant woman. But a surprise awaited her: Joseph would marry her, because a dream had revealed to him that Mary's pregnancy was of the Holy Spirit. Do you look for guidance in your dreams? When did you last have a dream with implicit guidance?

ILLUMINATIONS

We possess nothing in this world except the power to say *I*. A mere chance can strip us of everything. And that is what we have to give to God. In other words: Ourselves. There is absolutely no other free act that is given us to achieve—only the gift of oneself.[23]

—*Simone Weil, French philosopher (1909–1943)*

The background of the Magnificat is the tragic character of a world that is unjust. But . . . the mercy of God is not reserved for the end time alone. The mercy of God will not allow the wound to fester. The mercy of God takes historical forms, is made concrete in actions that transform the interplay of forces. The proud, with the power in their hands, the wealthy, do not have the last word. They think they have, but the divine justice is already upon them, in history itself. They will be stripped of their power. The mask will be torn away from their proud faces, and they will be sent away empty-handed (Luke 1:51–53).[24]

—*Leonardo Boff, Brazilian liberation theologian (1938–)*

. . . Mary of Nazareth, while completely devoted to the will of God, was far from being a timidly submissive woman or one whose piety was repellant to others; on the contrary, she was a woman who did not hesitate to proclaim that God vindicates the humble and the oppressed, and removes the powerful people of this world from their powerful positions (cf. Luke 1:51–53). [Mary] "stands out among the poor and the humble of the Lord," a woman of strength, who experienced poverty and suffering, flight and exile. (cf. Matthew 2:13–23)

—*Pope Paul VI (served 1963–1978)*

Be grateful for unknown blessings already on their way.
—*Native American, traditional*

PRAYERS

O, God,
help me to believe
the truth about myself—
no matter how beautiful it is![25]
—*Macrina Wiederkehr, contemporary Benedictine writer*

Alleluia!
Praise God in his sanctuary;
praise him in the vault of heaven,
praise him for his mighty deeds;
praise him for his own greatness.
Praise him with dance and tambourines;

Praise him with pipe and strings;
praise him with clashing cymbals,
praise him with clanging cymbals!
Let everything that breathes
sing praise to the LORD.
Alleluia!
—*Psalm 150*

O LORD, my heart is not proud
nor do I have arrogant eyes.
I am not engrossed in ambitious matters,
nor in things too great for me.

I have quieted and stilled my soul
like a weaned child on its mother's lap;
like a contented child is my soul.
Hope in the LORD, O Israel,
now and forever.
—*Psalm 131*

O, Mary, mother of Christ and of the family of God, help us in our evangelical ministry. We think of you in a special way because of your perfect gratitude in the words you spoke when your cousin Elizabeth, the mother of John the Baptizer, called you "blessed among women." You never became complacent in your blessedness, but focused your thoughts on all women and men. Yes, you thought of everyone, but you had a special preference for the poor, the same preference that your son would have one day. . . . O Mary, lend us your voice! Sing with us! Beg your son to accomplish in us, in all their fullness, his father's plans.[26]

—*Dom Helder Camera, Brazilian bishop and social activist (1910–2000)*

FREEING THE CREATIVE SPIRIT

This exercise invites you to dialogue with the Hail Mary. If you journal, write in your journal; or use a pencil and a U.S. letter-sized or metric A4-sized sheet of paper, or compose on your computer.

Write the Hail Mary in a nine-line format as it appears in Step 1, page 57, leaving several lines of space between each line of the prayer.

Begin your dialogue by slowly and prayerfully reading the first line. Then write your own prayerful response beneath it. When you are ready, read the second line, and respond to it in the same prayerful manner. Continue in the same way with each verse, including the ninth, which consists of only one word: Amen—a richly important word, echoing Mary's reply to Gabriel, "Let it be," "So be it," "May it be so."

This is a wonderful practice to repeat silently to yourself with new responses each time; or you can use a different prayer, such as the Magnificat or any of your favorite prayers, perhaps one you yourself have written.

STEP 4
THE NATIVITY

Mary Gives Birth to Jesus
(Luke 2:1–7)

LISTENING TO SCRIPTURE

In those days a decree went out from Caesar Augustus that all the world should be enrolled. This was the first enrollment, when Quirinius was governor of Syria. And all went to be enrolled, each to his own city. And Joseph also went up from Galilee, from the city of Nazareth, to Judea, to the city of David, which is called Bethlehem, because he was of the house and lineage of David, to be enrolled with Mary, his betrothed, who was with child. And while they were there, the time came for her to be delivered. And she gave birth to her first-born son and wrapped him in swaddling cloths, and laid him in a manger, because there was no place for them in the inn. (Luke 2:1–7)

IMAGINING THE STORY

It is December of the year we call 1, late in the third trimester of Mary's pregnancy, and careful plans have been made for the local midwife and women in Mary's family to help her deliver the baby. But dreaded news arrives, a message so important that soldiers of the Roman Empire have carried it on horseback almost a hundred miles from Damascus to Galilee. The imperial order states that a census is being taken, and everyone must register in person in his native town, which for Mary and Joseph means an eighty-mile journey to Bethlehem. They set out almost immediately, Joseph on foot, worried about his wife; Mary, heavy and uncomfortable, swaying on a thin donkey's back. Food is scarce, the night is cold, and the journey feels endless to them both. Imagine yourself in Mary's place. How would you feel?

Imagine that at a considerable distance before Bethlehem, Mary's water breaks, and she feels the first traces of pain. Labor has begun. Struggling to hide his fear, Joseph reassures her that Bethlehem is not far, and he will soon find a suitable place for her to labor and deliver her child. An hour passes before a searing pain sweeps across her body, announcing that contractions have begun in earnest. What do you imagine it is like for her to be in labor riding on a sluggish donkey's back, not knowing where she is or will be when the last contraction comes?

Imagine that many hours later, when the outskirts of Bethlehem finally come into sight, you see Mary slumped on the animal's back, obviously in excruciating pain and too exhausted to breathe a sigh of relief. Joseph, too, suffers acutely; he blames himself for their predicament and is mortified that he has failed to provide for his wife at a time like this. He is desperate to find the privacy of a room to alleviate at least some of her misery. It is hard enough to have to give birth in Bethlehem, far from home, with no women to help her, no midwife with soothing ointments and herbs, but the situation grows even more dire. The only shelter Joseph finds is a cold, dark stable by an inn, and he carries Mary inside. Anguish almost overwhelms him. Chances of both Mary and the baby surviving are slim.

How do you imagine this birthing room? Are there animals? If so, what kinds? What do you hear? What will Mary eat and drink? After she delivers, how will she manage to clean and dress the baby?

Can you imagine what this must be like for Joseph? Does he know how to deliver a baby? What kind of prayer is he probably saying? Perhaps he recalls Yahweh's promise in Isaiah 43:2,

"When you pass through the waters, I will be with you."

What is it like for you to be there? What are you feeling? What can you do to comfort the young couple? What are you praying?

More hours pass, and at last Mary gives birth to a perfect little boy, her youth, strength, and faith having brought them both safely through the grueling day. Now the whole atmosphere in the stable is transformed: everyone weeps with relief and joy. Jesus the Christ is now in the world. Picture the love on Joseph's face as he tenderly places the infant on Mary's chest. Imagine Mary in this instant of bonding with her baby. Can you visualize the light that artists through the ages have tried to depict shining on Mary's face and on the baby's entire body?

Are you aware of the sacredness of this historic moment? Do you truly grasp that the entrance of Mary's child into the world is changing the whole meaning and purpose of human life? Nothing will ever be the same again, because of him. What would you like to say to the new parents? What do they say to you?

MEDITATIONS

On the day before the Nativity—the day we celebrate on December 24—Mary is ready for the great transition that will complete her life as a girl and inaugurate her life as a woman. Over the course of the next day or so, her body will instinctively do wondrous things that no force on earth can accomplish, engaging a miraculous complexity of hormones so she can release into the world the precious being who has been growing inside her womb all these months. The Nativity will mark the greatest day of Mary's life. After her long period of waiting—three-quarters of an entire year—this incomparable transition from pre-motherhood to motherhood will occur in a single short but powerful day.

From the first day of her journey with her son, Mary will see how the heart expands when one has a child—expands and continues expanding, like a full moon always growing more full. The baby will open a new doorway to her husband's soul, allowing a vision of his own enlarging heart to come into view. As in the case of all loving parents, our own or ourselves, a relationship that on one

day is a two-way road becomes on the next a blessed trinity
of lovers meeting at new depths.

Between the holy sacraments of marriage and baptism,
there should be an eighth: the sacrament of giving birth.
For Catholics, each of life's most important moments, seven
transitional passages from birth through death, are blessed
and made holy by an appropriate sacrament. There is one
notably significant omission, however, the unfathomably
sacred event of giving birth. Although miracles, mysteries,
awe, and wonder surround the whole process of conceiving,
carrying, and delivering a child; although horrific pain
marks the event for the mother and the newborn undergoes
a traumatic entry the world; although countless tears of
pain and joy are shed and an entire team of people is
needed to help with the birth; despite all this, there is no
sacrament to honor the event.

How wonderful it would be for the parents' ordeal to be
honored by the Church! How life affirming to recognize
and celebrate the glorious changes that have been taking
place in the mother's body for nine months. What beauty
and peace a sacramental ritual could bring to the couple
and their waiting families before the baby's arrival, which
may be accomplished safely, or with difficulty, or even with
death and tragedy. Through the sacrament of baptism, the
infant will be joyfully welcomed into the faith community,
but something more than this is needed. A sacrament of
Giving Birth would add a dimension of sanctity that

would strengthen family bonding with the newborn and one another. Most important, it would deepen the world's awareness of Mary's experience of pregnancy and the birthing process, while helping millions of women to feel close to her during their own experiences of becoming mothers. Instead of carrying amulets and good-luck symbols into the birthing room, as many do today, women might recover the ancient custom of bringing with them a small statue of Mary.

Wonders and signs accompany the birth of Mary's baby, and wise men travel great distances just to look at him. Yet Mary's life with her infant son is in many ways no different from that of any other loving parent. From one day to the next, her whole life becomes devoted to taking care of a child, of someone other than herself, who now comes first, and for years if not decades to come, her universe will revolve around his laughter and tears. All the pleasures and delights parents feel just watching their child will highlight her day while she goes about the hard work involved in caring for a child. Like mothers across time, Mary will feed Jesus milk created in her own body, sew him swaddling clothes and blankets, change and bathe him, and comfort him with tender lullabies. She will give him her own herbal remedies when he falls sick, and later will cook his favorite foods for him and hold his hand while they walk to the village well. Even when Jesus arrives at the height of the terrible twos, her great heart will be incapable of constriction or of anything but love.

There will be the added responsibility of teaching Jesus good manners, setting limits, and explaining how to get along with other children. Mary will call on all her resources of intuition and intelligence, wisdom and love, to give her son the unbroken nurturing every human being deserves. Joseph, too, will pour all his abilities, his spiritual sensitivity, and his great depth of character into helping Mary raise Jesus while protecting and providing for his family. As a religiously observant man, Joseph will take Jesus to synagogue, pray with him at home, and help him with the Scriptures. When Jesus is old enough to learn a trade, Joseph will teach him his own woodworking skills.

The spiritual teachings in Step 4 are intended for all of us: women who have given birth, men called to fatherhood, all other women and men who find in the story of Jesus' birth a message about our own need for rebirth. Anglican priest Herbert O'Driscoll puts it this way:

> In jobs, careers, relationships, there comes a time when the waters of fullness pass; we feel a dryness, or emptiness, a realization that we must act or we will taste something of death. We must decide to set about being born toward the next stage of existence. . . .
>
> Often quite unexpected, we find ourselves helped toward giving birth to things we did not know lay within us, and the experience enables us to continue on the road to whatever Bethlehem we are bound for.[27]

Birthing the potential in our own souls is one of the most wonderful ways to emulate Mary. When we feel the firmest certitude that there is nothing inside ourselves, there is nothing to do, and we ourselves are nothing, it is time to go into labor. Something inside us is struggling to be born that must be midwifed into existence. Unlike the birth of a child, who arrives on no schedule but its own, our bringing something new into being is a choice. The creative spirit must be freed to put the best of ourselves into life. May we people of resurrection faith remember that there is always more to come.

REFLECTION QUESTIONS

- When have you had a birth experience? Do you think we are frequently reborn over the course of a Christian life? Explain.

- When have you served as midwife to another person's birth? Explain.

- Who served as midwife during one of your own rebirth experiences? Explain.

- This step on *The Way of Mary* offers a strong model of family bonding. A loving mother and a committed husband who are devoted to one another's well-being tenderly care for a child. What other signs of family strength do you notice in this story? Is there something in that image that you could bring into your own family, friendships, or community?

- Mary had to give birth far from home because of a

whim of the Roman emperor. Where in today's world do you see pregnant women displaced or maltreated?

ILLUMINATIONS

You have come, my beloved,
the clouds are gone;
The wind is silent.
The sun appears,
and the trees are green.
—from a song by *Tinh Thuy, Vietnamese Buddhist poet,*
    Plum Village, France, contemporary [28]

This day Mary has become for us
the heaven that births God.
In her has God grown small,
to make us great.[29]
—*St. Ephrem, Syrian monk (ca. 306–373)*

We, too, are Christ's mother when we carry him in our heart.[30]
    —*St. Francis of Assisi, beloved founder of the Franciscans*
    (ca. 1182–1226)

. . . though he was rich, for your sake he became poor,
that you, through his poverty, might become rich.
—*2 Corinthians 8:9*

This gentle loving child was born in a stable while his mother was on a journey to show all pilgrims how to be reborn in the stable of self-understanding. There, by grace, we find Christ birthed in our own souls.[31]

—*St. Catherine of Siena (1330–1444)*

Suddenly there was with the angel a multitude of the heavenly host, praising God and saying,

"Glory to God in the highest.

And on earth peace

among men of good will."

—*(Luke 2:13–14)*

PRAYERS

O True God,

I wake up today invoking your name and Holy Mary's,

for the running star has risen over Jerusalem,

and teaches me to say:

Arise in joy,

all you who love God,

daylight has come,

and the night has gone its way.[32]

—*Folquet of Marseilles, twelfth-century bishop*

Come, let us sing to the LORD,
let us make a joyful sound
to the Rock of our salvation.
Let us come before him giving thanks,
with music and songs of praise.

For the LORD is the great God,
the great King above all gods.

In his hand are the depths of the earth
and the mountain heights.
The sea is his, for he made it,
and his hand shaped the dry land.

Come and worship; let us bow down,
kneel before the LORD, our Maker.
He is our God, and we his people;
the flock he leads and pastures.

Would that today you heard his voice! . . .
—*Psalm 95*

FREEING THE CREATIVE SPIRIT

List five blessings you have received over the course of
your life. Think about today, yesterday, this season, this
year, then past years. Include people, events, milestones,
unforgettable days, and so on. Look also for blessings
in disguise, apparent hardships or misfortunes that had

good results. When you have written down five, add five additional blessings to your list. After those are recorded, add five more. Continue the blessings, listing them in increments of five as long as you wish, until you reach twenty; include more if you have time.

If you find this exercise to be difficult, it might help to broaden your definition of a blessing; it is not the same as a miracle. Remind yourself that the Spirit of Christ works through surprises, and many are ordinary, daily events that arrive in small packages. Not every gift of God has to be hugely significant. A friend of mine makes a twenty-minute pilgrimage to two beautiful magnolia trees each spring when they blossom, and she considers those two trees to be one of the great blessings in her life.

As the poet Eileen Caddy has observed, "The more blessings you count, the more they increase." Because the more we count, the more refined our awareness becomes. To enhance your awareness of the sacred in your life, of the reality and power of grace, try repeating this exercise in the future, recording blessings not on your previous list.

PONDERING THINGS IN THE HEART

Mary Thinks Deeply about Profound Events
(Luke 2:19, 51)

LISTENING TO SCRIPTURE

[T]he shepherds said to one another, "Let us go to Bethlehem and see this event that the Lord has made known to us." So they hurried away and found Mary and Joseph, and the baby lying in the manger. When they saw the child they repeated what they had been told about him, and everyone who heard it was astonished at what the shepherds said to them. As for Mary, she treasured all these things and pondered them in her heart. (Luke 2:15b–19)

IMAGINING THE STORY

Mary is asleep in the run-down stable in Bethlehem where she gave birth to Jesus. Joseph sits on the ground on a well-worn mat close to his wife and to the small wooden manger that usually holds food for animals but today substitutes for a cradle. Can you picture yourself there with the family? What are you doing? If you are sitting on the ground, what is that like? Is there any covering to sit on? Is the room quiet? What background noises can you hear? What can you see? Where are the animals? What is the source of light in the stable? How does Mary appear after yesterday's physical ordeal?

Imagine yourself having a conversation with Joseph. What do you say? What does he reply? Continue the conversation in your mind as long as you wish.

Now imagine the sound of people approaching. Startled, you look toward the large gate just as it opens, and a group of shepherds in patched, coarse woolen robes appears in the doorway. How do they look? They tell you a startling story about an apparition of an angel who told them such amazing things about a boy just born in Bethlehem that they felt compelled to come see him for themselves. Picture the shepherds as they look toward the infant. What do you imagine the shepherds saying to one another? Are they bothered by the extreme poverty of the environment? Watch as the shepherds draw closer to the baby and kneel down. What are their facial expressions and body language?

Mary is standing up now, wide awake, pensive and silent, and everything about her reveals fulfillment and joy, despite her obvious exhaustion. Warm light in her weary eyes speaks of overwhelming love for her husband and her tiny son. Picture her as she turns toward the shepherds. What does she say to the shepherds? How do they respond? Now it is your turn to speak to the shepherds: What do you tell or ask them? What is their reply? Imagine that Mary invites everyone to kneel on the ground close to Jesus to pray. What is her prayer?

MEDITATIONS

Artists do not often portray Mary as a deep thinker like Mary Magdalene and St. Jerome. But the truth is that she was a woman with a questioning mind as well as a questing heart, who wanted to understand what was happening in both the outer world of unplanned events and the inner, spiritual world of insight and prayer. The New Testament tells us more than once that she paused to reflect for a long time on her experience. Perhaps she influenced the Desert Fathers and Mothers of centuries to come, who would leave the cities of the Roman Empire to meditate in this way, in solitude and silence.

Even before the age of fourteen, when Gabriel came and she consecrated her life to high and holy purposes, Mary had mastered the sacred art of pondering things in the heart. For this is the self-possessed way she comported herself when the angel dropped into her life, like a lightning bolt out of the blue, with a shocking invitation. She kept her troubled feelings to herself to ponder her situation in the heart for a minute or so, preparing herself spiritually to talk things over with Gabriel.

It may be that Mary always walked a little more thoughtfully through her life than most of us, a little more present to everyday sights, sounds, and conversations, a little more ready to truly hear the voices in her environment and to penetrate the meaning of opaque events. It is clear that on any number of occasions and as a general rule, she took time to ponder in her heart before speaking or reacting.

What precisely does it mean *to ponder in the heart*?

It is important to realize that the word *heart* in the Hebrew of Mary's time had none of the sentimental connotations it has in English today, but referred to the whole self, to the entire person, body, mind, and spirit. It is unlikely that Mary spoke Hebrew as well as Aramaic, but as a Jewish woman of the time who lived among Jewish men who learned Hebrew in the Nazareth synagogue, she likely understood through them this broader meaning of the word *heart*. It would be a natural topic of conversation with her father, with Joseph, with other men in the family, and later with Jesus. Simply because the word is found in Scripture, it would be important to understand it clearly.

Of all the human behaviors Mary models for us, learning to "ponder in the heart" is the most important, the most personally transfiguring and world-healing, because it enables us to be the way we all at the depths of our souls long to be, and to do what we know in our depths is right and good for ourselves and for everyone else. All of which means living the Christian life of love. As a beautiful metaphor puts it, "We are all cups brimming over with love."[33] Our calling is to love. This is a hard vocation to respond to well, but grace is given to see us through.

That is an incontestable truth, the deep reality of our humanity. But before one can release such beautiful potential into life and apply love energy to all the ways we spend our time, much spiritual work needs to be accomplished. Providentially, the raw material for this work is provided through the profound and sacred events that sprinkle our days and nights—the numinous dreams, surprises, wise men, angelic beings, and synchronicity (inexplicable coincidences), to name but a few. When you learn to think about these things as Mary does, the most ordinary or boring event is a symbolic feast.

Wise women and men have always believed with the ancient Greeks that "the unexamined life is not worth living." Self-understanding is essential to find the presence of mind to pause and think with love about oneself and everything else. The gains in integrity and self-respect become literally visible in the body, for the stronger the spirit and the more alive the conscience, the more we carry ourselves with poise and presence.

There is a candle-lit room in the soul where our ancestors' wisdom is stored and a treasury of scriptures waits to be consulted. Like the library in a great medieval monastery, this is the place of retreat for practicing *The Way of Mary*. Ultimately, *pondering in the heart* means reflecting on things from a perspective of love, with the realization that God is close and involved in every experience. This way is not always easy. Sometimes charged events pile up in the soul like boulders, hard to move or make transparent and impossible to transmute into gold. That is the best time to invoke Mary's presence and ask her to help.

To keep your experience of thinking and love together, try saying over and over again in the silence of the soul, with Mary, "I love you; I love you; I love you." This is a prayer of the Christian saints and mystics, the holiest and most powerful prayer we can address to God.

REFLECTION QUESTIONS

- Mary's way of pondering in the heart is an example of spiritual practice even though it does not involve any outward physical activity. She thinks things through in the silence and presence of God's love. She holds an attitude of love and trust. When you are confronted with a problem or experience that calls for reflection, do you approach it as Mary did? Do you bring in your feelings, imagination, ideas, and memories? Think of an instance when you pondered things in the heart before speaking or acting. Think of a time when you wish you had.

- Do you have a concern today that you would like to resolve—with a relationship, at work, a memory in need of healing, a failure, loss, or dream? Can you begin to think about your concern as Mary would, with an attitude of love, placing your trust in God?

- Explain in your own words what it means to ponder things in the heart. Why is this a spiritual practice? How do you bring God into it?

- How could you use Mary's way of pondering to help others? Could you share it with friends and family members, especially children?

ILLUMINATIONS

In every generation, [wisdom] passes into holy souls,
and makes them friends of God, and prophets.
—*Wisdom 7:27b*

Lord, not you, it is I who am absent.
—*Denise Levertov, English poet (1923–1998)*

Be aware of the time, the place and the circumstances,
but more than that, be aware of yourself, your soul, what
is happening in your body in the moment. It is not only a
question of seeing things as they are, but of seeing yourself as
you really are.
—*Indian wisdom, traditional*

To complain is always refusal of what is.
—*Source unknown*

Court [wisdom] with all your soul,
and with all your might keep her ways;
go after her and seek her;
she will reveal herself to you;
once you hold her, do not let her go.
For in the end you will find rest in her
and she will take the form of joy for you.
—*Ecclesiasticus 6:26–28*

Waking up this morning, I smile. Twenty-four brand new hours are before me. I vow to live fully in each minute and to look at all beings with eyes of compassion.[34]

—*Thich Nhat Hanh, contemporary Vietnamese Buddhist monk*

Leave [immaturity] and live,
and walk in the way of insight.
—*Source unknown*

Wisdom is more precious than pearls,
and nothing else is so worthy of desire.
—*Proverbs 8:11*

The beginning of wisdom is this:
Seek wisdom.
—*Proverbs 4:7*

PRAYERS

PRAYER TO OUR LADY OF APARECIDA

(a title given to Mary as the patron saint of Brazil)

Lady Aparecida, a son of yours who belongs to you unreservedly—*totus tuus*—called by the mysterious plan of Providence to be the Vicar of your son on earth, wishes to address you at this moment. He recalls with emotion, because of the brown color of this image of yours, another image of yours, the Black Virgin of Jasna Gora.

Mother of God and our Mother, protect the church, the pope, the bishops, the priests and all the faithful people; welcome under your protecting mantle men and women religious, families, children, young people, and their educators.

Health of the sick and Consoler of the afflicted, comfort those who are suffering in body and soul; be the light of those who are seeking Christ, the Redeemer of all; show all people that you are the mother of our confidence.

Queen of Peace and Mirror of Justice, obtain peace for the world; ensure that . . . and all countries may have lasting peace, that we will always live together as brothers and sisters and as children of God.

Our Lady Aparecida, bless all your sons and daughters who pray and sing to you here and elsewhere. Amen.

—Pope John Paul II (served 1978–2005)

PRAYER FOR SPIRITUAL GROWTH

Dear Lord, you see how we become used to everything. Once I gladly took up your service with the firm intent of being wholly surrendered to you. But since every day brings nearly the same thing over and over again, it seems to me that my prayer has been circumscribed. I limit myself to just what seems necessary for the task at hand so that in the end my spirit has assumed the size of this small task. I ask you to help me not to narrow myself in this way; expand me again; give me some of the power of Mary's consent, which waits in readiness for the entire divine will, which is always as all-embracing as it was when first pronounced and which is daily conformed anew.

She may have been glad or afraid or hopeful, weary of the daily work or led to the cross: always she stood before you as at first, accepting everything you said, hoping to do everything you wished. Behind every one of your wishes, even the smallest, she saw the great, unlimited will of the Father which you, the Son, were fulfilling.[35]

—*Adrienne von Speyr, Swiss Protestant physician and mystic (1902–1967)*

FREEING THE CREATIVE SPIRIT

Philip Armstrong, CSC, offers an imaginative approach to one of the most popular prayers of all time, the Rosary. Each decade of the Rosary is accompanied by a mystery, and traditionally there have been three sets of mysteries: the Joyful, Sorrowful, and Glorious Mysteries. In 2002, Pope John Paul II added a forth group, the Luminous Mysteries, or Mysteries of Light. Inspired by Pope John Paul's example, Brother Armstrong created a number of alternative mysteries, and recommends that we do the same, occasionally substituting our own mysteries for the customary ones. They must be suitable for prayerful reflection, of course. Among Brother Armstrong's alternative mysteries are the Golden Rule mysteries. These are five New Testament verses in which Jesus teaches reciprocal behaviors, as does the Golden Rule.[36] They are as follows:

(1) Be compassionate, just as your Father is compassionate (Luke 6:36);
(2) Do not judge, and you will not be judged (Luke 6:37);
(3) Do not condemn, and you will not be condemned (Luke 6:37);
(4) Forgive, and you will be forgiven (Luke 6:37);
(5) Give, and it will be given to you (Luke 6:38a).

One of my own alternatives is to use the Rosary as intercessory prayer, dedicating each decade to a person I love (a different person with each decade), or to five people in need. Another approach is to meditate on a problem in a specific nation, such as global warming in the United States or war in the Sudan, moving to a new nation with each decade. Yet another group of mysteries could be taken from *The Way of Mary*. Choose any five steps, presumably five that you find especially moving, and meditate on one with each decade. The next time you pray, select five different steps.

A powerful set of alternative mysteries that Brother Armstrong recommends is the Rites of Passage Mysteries. These consist of five major transitions in one's life, such as the following:

(1) A meaningful challenge;
(2) a transfiguring spiritual experience;
(3) another person's helpful and lasting influence;
(4) experiencing the real meaning of life and death; and
(5) deep awareness of your own gifts.[37]

To practice freeing the creative spirit today, look back on your own life and select five events that you can use to create your own Rites of Passage Mysteries following the outline given above. Then prayerfully ponder one mystery with each decade as you pray the Rosary.

SIMEON'S PROPHECY

A Sword Will Pierce Mary's Heart
(Luke 2:25–35)

LISTENING TO SCRIPTURE

When the time came for their purification according to the law of Moses, they brought him up to Jerusalem to present him to the Lord. . . . Now there was a man in Jerusalem whose name was Simeon, and this man was righteous and devout, looking for the consolation of Israel, and the Holy Spirit was upon him. And it had been revealed to him by the Holy Spirit that he should not see death before he had seen the Lord's Christ. And inspired by the Spirit he came into the temple; and when the parents brought in the child Jesus, to do for him according to the custom of the law, he took him up in his arms and blessed God and said:

> *"Lord, now let your servant depart in peace,*
> *according to your word;*
> *for my eyes have seen your salvation*
> *which you have prepared in the presence of all peoples,*
> *a light for revelation to the Gentiles,*
> *and for glory to your people Israel."*

And his father and his mother marveled at what was said about him; and Simeon blessed them and said to Mary his mother,

"This child is destined to be the downfall and rise of many in Israel, a sign that will be opposed—and you yourself shall be pierced with a sword—so that the thoughts of many hearts may be laid bare." (Luke 2:22–35)

IMAGINING THE STORY

It is February 2 of the year we name 2, and Mary's time of separation from society is drawing to a close. According to Jewish custom, she was religiously clean a week after giving birth, but thirty-three days of additional separation are required to complete purification observances. (Eighty days are customary after the birth of a girl.) Now that Jesus is turning forty days old, he can be brought to Jerusalem for a sacred ritual that has been celebrated by Mary's and Joseph's families for many generations. The couple will present their son to a priest in the majestic temple, the heart of their world, and offer two birds as a living sacrifice.

In your imagination, picture yourself journeying with the family to Jerusalem, pausing on the Mount of Olives at a favorite outlook. Allow yourself to relish the heart-stopping view of the temple, the beauty of its white marble walls and tower gleaming in the sun. You can see why it is one of the architectural wonders of its day, bigger than the biggest Roman palace, longer than six New York City blocks, broader than the future basilica in Trier. Imagine you have a close-up view through modern binoculars of visitors pouring through the temple compound, marveling at the great staircase, archways, gardens, plentiful pools of water defying the desert climate. What do you feel as you ponder the magnificence of this scene? Do you wish that, like the high priest alone, you could enter the Holy of Holies where Yahweh is said to dwell?

Is it conceivable to you that the tiny baby Mary holds in her arms will one day shake this temple to its foundations by exposing corruption, questioning priestly authority, assailing the whole religious establishment for abusing the poor, for animal sacrifice, for their very concept of God?[38] Surely no one could suspect that this innocent baby will be killed for revealing that God is love, and that the authentic temple of God lies in the human heart.

And yet, there is one person with the vision to see what lies ahead: Simeon, a living prophet, and he happens to be in the temple when you arrive with the holy family. Now a very old man, he approaches Mary. How do you imagine him: dressed in rags, bent over, with a craggy face and blazing eyes, or totally different from such an appearance? Watch as he reaches out his hands for the baby, and Mary hands Jesus to him. Simeon recites an exquisite prayer of perfect fulfillment and readiness now known as the *Nunc Dimittis* or "Song of Simeon," telling God that his life's purpose has been fulfilled by learning that the Messiah has come in Mary's child. How do you imagine Mary feels listening to Simeon's beautiful affirmation? Simeon echoes God's promise made on the holiest day of her life some ten months ago, when she became pregnant. Simeon's insights resound like a reaffirmation of that message for Mary to cling to should she ever need reassurance about her child's true identity. What does Mary feel at this moment? Joseph is regarded here as the baby's father: how must he feel?

Sadly, there is little time for Mary and Joseph to rejoice in the prophet's words, as he turns to Mary and prophesies extreme suffering. How does Mary look when she hears this? Does she believe Simeon? What does her body language tell you? What does she do? It wouldn't be like Mary to turn away from the old man and rush to the exit. Does she remain silent? If not, what does she say? Does Joseph say anything? Would you like to speak with Mary, Joseph, or Simeon?

MEDITATIONS

Simeon's beautiful prayer, the *Nunc Dimittis,* opens with words that have touched a deep chord in the human heart across time: "Lord, now let your servant depart in peace. . . ." This beloved prayer is most frequently offered when light is waning at either the close of a day or the closing of a life.

One might wish Simeon had stopped there, so Mary and Joseph could leave the temple as happily as they entered it. Instead, no sooner had he finished thanking God for his life's fulfillment in the vision of the Christ than the prophet's face darkened, and his tone grew ominous. Simeon foresaw prophetically that extreme suffering lay ahead for this tiny child and for his mother. He saw the image of a heavy sword cutting into the body of Jesus, then into Mary's heart; and he told Mary what he saw.

It is tempting to dismiss the old man as mad[39] for interjecting a threat of violence on such a joyful day as a child's presentation in the temple. Interrupting the ancient presentation rites in this way shattered the young family's peace of mind, just as it would disturb a baptism today. But neither the exquisite beauty nor the enduring spiritual influence of the *Nunc Dimittis* could come from a lunatic. Unlike pagan oracles, sibyls, and soothsayers who "prophesied" in drug-induced trances and artificial stupors or under the influence of toxic fumes, like the Oracle of Delphi, Simeon was genuine. He was one of those rare holy men and women of God in the Jewish and Christian traditions who truly see into eternity. And what Simeon saw is that Jesus was the suffering servant foretold in the Scriptures, a future king, but not in the sense of palaces and power. This king is from all eternity a crucified God.

But why does Simeon tell a young woman with a baby in her arms on one of the most joyful occasions of a new family's life that terrible affliction lies ahead? Why not keep such dark knowledge to himself? In part, to prepare the way of the Lord. In part, to fulfill the Scriptures. In part, to speak through the centuries to all men and women about impermanence. Neither today's joy nor tomorrow's suffering lasts very long in the grand scheme of things, nor does anything else, until we enter eternity and fall in love forever with the vision of God.

Prophets are sent to disturb us with the truth, to jolt and shock us out of inaction, denial, disbelief, and time-wasting distractions while bombed cities burn. Simeon did indeed speak a disturbing truth, but it was not for Mary. He warned the people all around her, ourselves, and all people to come, of grenade-like forces that can explode in our own hands. Mary's baby had come to give joy, yet men, who were created only a little less than the angels, would execute him in the cruelest possible way.

On this sixth step along *The Way of Mary*, an event that she would ponder in her heart for decades to come, Mary realized that she did not yet understand the full implications of her calling. She had no idea that raising a child could entail so much pain, nor did she know of her central role in the divine tragedy that had been unfolding within her, through her, and around her, and was well underway. What mother could bear to think that she will outlive her child and watch him die, even with the certitude that he will be reborn? Mary would endure many sleepless nights as a result of her charged encounter with Simeon, but she took a giant leap forward in understanding her son, his hidden nature, and his staggering destiny.

She is known as the church's first christological thinker,[40] the first person to reflect on the Christ, because of the many years she spent at Jesus' side, watching and listening to him, reflecting on what he said and did, weighing his choice of friends, pondering his fevered devotion to

God. Here, once again, she modeled a vitally important behavior for us.

Simply thinking about Jesus can take us far.

REFLECTION QUESTIONS

- To present a boy in the temple in Mary's time, parents were obligated to purchase a living animal, such as a sheep or goat, or, if they were poor, two birds for a priest to kill as a living sacrifice to Yahweh. Jesus attacked this practice for placing an unessential burden on the poor. What other reason(s) can you give for Jesus' condemnation of these rites? What did Jesus recommend in place of animal sacrifice?[41]

- Have you ever met a person whose eyes revealed holiness? If so, how did meeting that person affect you? What was the outcome?

- Simeon blessed God before speaking the *Nunc Dimittis* and blessed Mary and Joseph before delivering his prophetic warning. Is the meaning of the blessing similar in both instances?

- Does Simeon's warning include a reminder that no one's life consists entirely of joys and pleasures without ordeals? Can you think of a person whom you see as "coasting" through life without hardships? Do you believe today that most people have a more or less equal share of blessings and difficulties, or do you find a significant discrepancy among individuals and peoples?

- What do you imagine as Simeon's most lasting impact on Mary? How might she have grown in self-understanding by reflecting on his message? How do you think the prophet affected Joseph? What is the lasting impact of the story on you?

ILLUMINATIONS

> I had heard of you by the hearing of the ear,
> but now my eyes see you.
> —*Job 42:5*

> Now that my house has been burned to the ground,
> I have an unobstructed view of the rising moon.
> —*Buddhist wisdom, traditional*

> There is nothing—no thing, no person, no experience, no thought, no joy or pain—that cannot be harvested and used for nourishment on our journey to God.[42]
> —*Macrina Wiederkehr, contemporary Benedictine writer*

> See beauty in the midst of misery, hope in the center of pain.
> —*Henri Nouwen, twentieth-century priest and writer born in Holland*

What one fully understands cannot be God.

—*St. Augustine of Hippo,*
Doctor of the Church (354–430)

Trust in the LORD.

—*Psalm 4:5*

PRAYERS

I rejoiced with those who said to me,
"Let us go to the house of the LORD!"
And now we have set foot
within your gates, O Jerusalem!

Jerusalem, just like a city,
where everything falls into place!
There the tribes go up.
The tribes of the LORD, the assembly of Israel,
to give thanks to the LORD's name.
There stand the courts of justice,
the offices of the house of David.

Pray for the peace of Jerusalem:
"May those who love you prosper!
May peace be within your walls
and security within your citadels!"

—*Psalm 122*[43]

PRAYER TO OUR LADY OF COMBERMERE

(a title given to Mary in Combermere, Ontario)

O, Mary, you desire so much to see Jesus loved. Since you love me, this is the favor which I ask of you: to obtain for me a great personal love of Jesus Christ. You obtain from your son whatever you please; pray for me that I may never lose the grace of God, that I may increase in holiness and perfection from day to day, and that I may faithfully and nobly fulfill the great calling in life which your divine son has given me. By that grief which you suffered at Calvary when you beheld Jesus dying on the cross, obtain for me a happy death, that by loving Jesus and you, my Mother, on earth, I may share your joy in loving and blessing the Father, the Son, and the Holy Spirit forever in Heaven.

Our Lady of Combermere, pray for us.

—*Madonna House Apostolate, founded 1947 by*
   Catherine de Hueck Dougherty

We place ourselves in your keeping, Holy Mother of God.
Hear the prayer of your children in distress
and protect us all from danger,
O you who are so blessed.

—Sub tuum Praesidium, *the oldest extant hymn to Mary*

FREEING THE CREATIVE SPIRIT

Try your hand at creating a Mary garden. This doubly rich spiritual practice nurtures your closeness to Mary while taking you into the sacredness of the earth and the life force that causes seeds to burst out of their shells. Your garden can be located indoors or outdoors and be as simple or imaginative as you wish. It suffices to keep a fresh flower in a special bud vase reserved for Mary, perhaps on your Mary altar, surrounded by objects from nature. Some people grow special plants on a windowsill for a larger indoor garden. Others place a statue of Mary in an outdoor garden area dedicated to her. Depending on your climate, you could grow flowers familiar to Mary in Galilee, such as roses, lilies, anemones, and cyclamen; or herbs such as sage, cumin, or rosemary. Some people with considerable space grow a fruit or nut tree (or a grove of trees) such as a date palm, or an orange or a lemon tree.[44]

Literally hundreds of flowers have been associated with Mary. Artists often represent the angel Gabriel greeting Mary with a white lily in his hand to symbolize her incorruptibility. Saints such as St. Thérèse of Lisieux have told about sensing the fragrance of roses in the absence of real flowers, associating the sweetness with Mary. Our Lady of Guadalupe gave Juan Diego rose petals as evidence of her appearance. In the Middle Ages, bundles of herbs and flowers believed to have healing powers, such as periwinkle and thyme, were taken to the church on the feast of Mary's assumption to be filled with her power by a special blessing and incensing. They would be kept in the home for a year to promote health. Marigolds were planted close to the home to also ward off illness.

If you like, go online and search for Mary gardens, or check local resources and talk to other people for information. If you are close to Cape Cod, Massachusetts, you might like to visit the lovely Marian garden at St. Joseph's Church in Woods Hole. Said to be the first in the United States, the garden was planted in 1932, and is a wonderful place for a prayerful pilgrimage.

Pray while planting or arranging your Mary garden, especially by invoking Mary's closeness. Give full rein to your creativity and you will make something beautiful to nurture as part of your permanent spiritual practice.

MEETING THE PROPHET ANNA

A Woman Prophet
Proclaims the Greatness of Mary's Son
(Luke 2:36–38)

LISTENING TO SCRIPTURE

There was a prophet, Anna, the daughter of Phanuel, of the tribe of Asher. She was well on in years. Her days of girlhood over, she had been married for seven years before becoming a widow. She was now eighty-four years old and never left the Temple, serving God night and day with fasting and prayer. She came up at that very moment and began to praise God; and she spoke of the child to all who looked forward to the deliverance of Jerusalem. (Luke 2:36–38)

IMAGINING THE STORY

Picture yourself inside the spectacular Jerusalem temple with Mary, Joseph, and the infant Jesus. While you wait for the presentation ceremony to begin, observe a steady stream of people arriving at the temple with flailing birds, bleating calves, and other terrified animals to be sacrificed by blood-splattered priests as living offerings to Yahweh. In addition to presentation offerings, there are peace offerings, guilt offerings, thanksgiving offerings, and others. Mary and Joseph purchased two doves for Jesus' ritual. How do you feel seeing and hearing this procession of animals? What is it like for Mary?

As part of the rites of presentation, Joseph hands Jesus to the priest, who then gives him back. Picture yourself standing beside Joseph and notice the rich symbolic meaning of the gesture; for example, the suggestion that a child belongs to God and is only on loan to the parents for a time.

After the ceremony, an elderly woman renowned for her holiness comes over to Mary. She is the prophet Anna, and Mary is deeply moved to meet a woman of such *gravitas,* such depth and seriousness of purpose. Anna's prophetic gifts and character have been formed through half a century of widowhood made meaningful by her spirituality. As an elder, she has been allowed for many years to leave the confines of the women's court and go about the temple as she wishes, devoting her remaining time to worship.

In your imagination, look closely at this wise and ancient soul. Anna has eyes that seem to see into eternity. What is her voice like? Tender and gentle? Strong and firm? How else would you describe her? Sadly, her words are not recorded in the New Testament, but she knows in the spirit of prophecy who Jesus is. She sees, as did Simeon, that he is the Messiah. From this moment on, Anna will reveal to everyone who comes to the temple that the Savior has been born.

Imagine that you hear Mary speak to Anna. What does she say? What does Anna say in return? Allow the conversation to continue in your mind for a minute or two.

MEDITATIONS

Mary's meeting with Anna in the temple is one of the most beautiful and moving occasions of Mary's life. To her utter amazement, she finds herself at the side of a woman prophet, a holy woman, one renowned for the intensity of her spiritual practice, her moral authority, her breadth of vision, and her wisdom. Scripture does not record Anna's words, but it is inconceivable that no conversation took place between these two great female souls. It may be that Anna said sacred things to Mary that the young woman would remember all her life. It may be that when Jesus was a little boy, Mary often told him about meeting the great Anna. Perhaps she taught Anna's wisdom to Jesus, perhaps his parables retained a trace of the prophet's influence. (Certainly, the parables contained more than a trace of his mother's influence.)

Or it could be that Mary merely asked Anna to pray for her without engaging her in conversation? We do not know. But it is certain that this privileged encounter with a consecrated woman left an indelible mark on Mary's rapidly maturing heart. Now not just one but two prophets have reiterated to her the angel Gabriel's message about her son's divine identity.

When Anna looks down at the tiny child in Mary's arms, fully aware of who he is, it is as though she is seeing beyond the boundaries of space and time. It is evident that her gaze penetrates through Jesus' physical appearance to his divine identity. There are no revelatory signs, but Anna knows intuitively, in the Spirit, that this baby is the Anointed One of God. It is through the intensity of her spiritual practice in the temple and her faithfulness to her prophetic calling that she has been blessed with such gracious gifts. Anna is someone Mary can trust.

Anna is allowed to move about in the temple pursuing her spiritual goals. Like her contemporaries the Essenes, who retreated to caves to seek holiness, and like today's Christian nuns and monks, Anna has given her life completely to God. She is a holy and lovely example of surrender. Having let go of possessions, desires, and drives, she is free to live in and for God. What this magnificent woman cherishes in her old age, rather than wealth and pleasure, is dedication to a demanding, disciplined daily round of worship, fasting, and prayer.

The role Anna plays in the evolving Christian drama does not stop with Mary's meeting with her. On the contrary, Anna's prophetic insights about Jesus merely begin the holiest and most important stage of her life's work. What wins her lasting fame is her decision to tell everyone about Mary's son. Anna *proclaims* Jesus' birth. She does not keep to herself the advent of the Christ. She makes it known. She proclaims his coming to *all* who are looking for the Lord. In doing so, Anna makes a crucial contribution to the Christian story, spreading the word from her position of influence, helping to prepare the way for the world-shattering work to come. Anna is the first person of either sex in the Gospels to proclaim to the people the Messiah's arrival on earth. There is no mention in the New Testament of Simeon's playing a similar role. We do not know whether or not he did. It may be that he is ready to depart the temple and rest; or to depart this life and pass on to the next world[45] now that he has seen the Christ, the long-awaited fulfillment of his longing.

Anna is a woman we can imitate by telling others about the presence of Jesus the Christ in our hearts and in the world.

REFLECTION QUESTIONS

- How is Anna a model for young Mary? Do you think Mary will remember and think about her as one of the great gift givers of her life? When Jesus is growing up, what will Mary tell him about her? Can you imagine four-year-old Jesus saying, "Tell me an Anna story, Mama?"

- Anna's habit of fasting is a wonderful spiritual practice for coming closer to God. Have you tried fasting? What was the experience like? If you have never fasted for spiritual purposes, would you like to try it by substituting an hour of prayer for one meal? What do you think of the Jewish, Christian, and Muslim custom of fasting on a holy day, or in preparation for one?

- If you knew of a holy woman like Anna living today, would you go to her for advice on a pressing problem? If so, what issue would you like to ask her about? Try taking the same problem to Mary in prayer. Do you believe that a silent conversation with her might bring you precisely the answer you need?

- Anna has embraced the elder years as the richest time in life for spiritual growth; she seems to think the soul is more pregnant with possibilities in old age than ever before. Do you agree? If you are an elder, how could you enrich your spirituality? If a loved one of yours is in the last decades of life, how could you help him or her to develop more spiritual resources?

ILLUMINATIONS

> What is this flesh I purchased with my pains,
> This fallen star my milk sustains,
> This love that makes my heart's blood stop
> Or strikes a sudden chill into my bones
> And bids my hair stand up?
> —*William Butler Yeats, Irish poet (1865–1939)*[46]

> (Seek wisdom) with all your soul,
> and with all your strength keep her ways.
> —*Ecclesiasticus 6:26*

I taught myself
to live simply, wisely,
to look at the sky,
and pray.
—*Anna Akhmatova, Russian writer (1889–1966)* [47]

I am moving
Toward a new freedom
Born of detachment,
And a sweeter grace—
Learning to let go.
—May Sarton, *twentieth-century poet*

Be who you are,
and may you be blessed
in all that you are.
—*Rabbi Marcia Falk*

PRAYERS

Some of you I will hollow out.

I will make you a cave.

I will carve you so deep the stars will shine in your darkness.

You will be a bowl.

You will be the cup in the rock collecting rain. . . .

I will do this because the world needs the hollowness of you.

I will do this for the space that you will be.

I will do this because you must be large.

A passage.

People will find their way through you.

—*From "Mother Wisdom Speaks" by Christine Lore Webber*

For your kingdom to come, O Lord,

may the kingdom of Mary come.

—*St. Louis-Marie Grignion de Montfort, French mystic and priest*
(1673–1716)

FREEING THE CREATIVE SPIRIT

This practice is unfailingly reliable when we need to re-center ourselves in God's love. Since the spiritual journey tends to take us through stages of centering, de-centering, and re-centering, a practice that brings us back to the center is invaluable. Here is what you do:

Think back over your life, reflecting on people who have played a loving role in your life. Think of them as gift givers, and list them as they come to mind. Perhaps one of these gift givers helped you just by listening to you, while another gave you wise advice, and someone else said something beautiful or inspiring that you will never forget. If a child made something for you, be sure to include him or her, as well as people of all ages. It may be that some of the people on your list never knew that they gave you their love, and there may be people whom you met only once.

Keep in mind that people with the least material wealth may have the most to give away. (Elders sometimes belong in this category.) Maybe a person who belongs on your list opened a door for you to a better job or improve a relationship, or provided an opportunity for you to know yourself better, find your worth, get in touch with your real values, or to forgive or repent. One of the most important goals of this exercise is to discover what a large number of people have cared for you and served your needs.

When you prepare your list, write down the person's name, your age at the time, where you were, and what the gift was. When you have ten gift givers on your list, you may realize that there are many more people whom you could add. I suggest that you stop for now, as you have completed only the first half of the practice. You can always come back to it again and again.

Make a new list. This time, look back over your life for ten occasions when *you* were the gift giver, recording the name of the person, your age at the time, the place, and a word or two to describe the gift. Allow yourself to open your heart widely and see how much you have given to others, possibly without realizing it.

When you complete the two lists, reflect on the meaning of these events. What have you learned from this exercise?

Bring the practice to a close by spending a few minutes in prayer, thanking God for the twenty men, women, and children whom you have remembered today, and for the grace of being a gift giver yourself.

THE ESCAPE TO EGYPT

Mary and Joseph Become Political Refugees
to Save Jesus from Herod's Killings
(Matthew 2:13b–15)

LISTENING TO SCRIPTURE

Suddenly the angel of the Lord appeared to Joseph in a dream and said, "Get up, take the child and his mother with you, and escape into Egypt, and stay there until I tell you, because Herod intends to search for the child and to do away with him." So Joseph got up and, taking the child and his mother with him, left that night for Egypt, where he stayed until Herod was dead. This was to fulfill what the Lord had spoken through the prophet:

"I called my son out of Egypt." (Matthew 2:13–15)

IMAGINING THE STORY

In your imagination set the calendar to nine months before spring of the year 1, when Mary is only a few weeks pregnant. Place yourself in Nazareth with a deeply spiritual and sensitive man named Joseph, a tanned, slender, rather short woodworker who is hammering nails into a wagon. Look at the surroundings: What do you see? What do you hear? Do you smell food cooking?

Joseph tells you about a startling dream he had last night that told him to do exactly the opposite of what he wants to do. He was about to break his betrothal, even though betrothal is a binding agreement, unbreakable except for infidelity. But his fiancée is pregnant, obviously guilty of infidelity, and that is cause for the radical act of ending the commitment. He is indescribably ashamed of Mary, yet cannot bring himself to ignore a dream, a source of divine guidance, and begins to feel he must go through with marriage. Put yourself in Joseph's place. How do you feel about his dilemma? Would you break off the engagement or trust that God is working through the dream?

Now, move nine months forward; it is early winter in the year 2, and you are in Bethlehem. Joseph is a married man with a newborn child, and once again has a powerful dream. This dream wakes him in the middle of the night with a terrifying warning to take his wife and baby and flee the house immediately, as King Herod's men are coming to kill Jesus. He instantly awakens Mary and tells her the horrifying news. She throws their few clothes and a little flatbread and goat's cheese into a satchel, pours water into a few goatskins, and the family rushes out into the cold night on a desperate journey to a foreign land. Robbers haunt the dark roads they will be forced to travel tonight. In the morning they will be safer on well-maintained Roman roads patrolled by soldiers. Way stations will have to meet their meager needs, since there is no money for meals or rooms at inns along the way.

Mary, Joseph, and the baby have become homeless refugees.

What do you imagine it is like for a new mother to come so close to the murder of her child? How would you feel in her place? Mary has been driven out of her home, forced to leave behind her dream of returning to her home in Nazareth, her parents, family, lifelong friends, the community of women she talks with daily at the well. Her entire lifestyle and support system are gone. What is it like to hurry toward a foreign land with no clear destination and no one to greet you or give you shelter? Do you picture Mary worried that an arduous trip on foot so soon after childbirth will exhaust her, possibly decreasing her breast milk? Is she anxious that the baby will die from one of the contagious diseases so prevalent on the road? Or do you envision her as calm, drawing strength from prayer, trusting in God? What would you like to say to her? How does she reply?

MEDITATIONS

Mary's first real test of faith, her first experience of devastating suffering, comes in the middle of the night when she learns that the murderous tyrant ruling her land is determined to kill her child. And not only hers, but every baby under two in Bethlehem, since any one of them might be Jesus. Herod and his vast web of spies and informers have always been a distant threat, but now his soldiers are on the march, coming closer every minute, eager to start their slaughter. This shattering night, with death so close at hand, surpasses in sheer misery everything Mary will undergo raising her holy son—until the unsurpassable experience of his death. But faith planted as deeply as Mary's survives even such a harrowing and formidable test. She will be able to understand that even the horror of the killing of the Innocents, through a strange twist of divine providence, makes it possible for Jesus to fulfill God's plans for his public ministry and sacrificial death.

During the long journey to Egypt, the couple must be assailed by fears and worries about every aspect of their future. Wherever they settle, strange gods will be worshiped; an incomprehensible language will be spoken; it may be impossible to follow their dietary customs; and it will be difficult for Joseph to make a living. Had they been able to travel home to Nazareth, Mary would be surrounded by nurturing women eager to support her in the art of child-raising and teach her the mothering skills women pass from generation to generation. But in the new location, deprived of this precious treasury, Mary will be isolated and alone.

The plight of Mary and Joseph on that terrible night offers a vivid image of the misery that *tens of millions* of refugees suffer in our own time. Driven from their homes by violence and radical poverty, fleeing all the Herods who tyrannize nations across the world today, these people set out with essentially no place to go. They search for food, water, and a degree of safety they may never find, ending up in barren places where no one wants to be. Television and the Internet show images every day of huge, empty eyes staring out at nothing but broken bodies and minds that are never going to heal.

Because of this chapter in their lives, Mary, Joseph, and Jesus joined the endless waves of emigrants who crisscross the earth today fleeing violence and poverty. The holy family will always share in the sufferings of the many who journey in crates and cargo holds, in boxcars and the back of trucks, crossing hot deserts only to be trapped like animals and sent home.

How many mothers of newborns among today's millions of refugees and emigrants are fleeing, as Mary and Joseph did, to safeguard the lives of their children? There are too many to number, and no words are big enough to describe their pain. Mary's endurance of such a terrible time of testing and ordeal offers such people—and *all* people—a living archetype of a woman strengthened by hardship embraced in the light of faith.

A central spiritual teaching for us in Step 8 concerns compassion. Today's world is filled with eyes in every dimension and plane, so there is no escaping the sight of immigrants and refugees in the dark abyss of their suffering. May our spiritual practice today include prayer for Mary's intercession in these tragic lives. May our hearts be moved to pray daily for those in need in our own country and throughout the world. May we take action on their behalf, doing anything we can, wherever we are, to help alleviate their pain.

REFLECTION QUESTIONS

- Have you ever experienced feelings of fear and alienation such as those that Mary and Joseph suffered in a foreign country after being forced to leave their home? If so, how did you cope with those feelings? How did you adjust to the new situation? If you have not been involved in such an extremely challenging situation, but if one came about in the future, how do you imagine you would deal with your fear and alienation? What measures would you take to adapt to the newness? What aspects of your faith life would help you the most?

- How do you see Mary and Joseph dealing with the trauma of their loss and their alienation in Egypt? What did they do in order to adjust to the new reality?

- Joseph's trusting attitude toward life was shaped by prayer, Scripture study, religious observance, and belief in divine guidance. How might this strong spiritual background affect his experience as a refugee? Since Mary had similar faith, how might they have strengthened and comforted one another during their life in exile?

- Do you pray for the people seeking food and shelter all over the world today? There are almost forty million refugees in Africa, the Middle East, Latin America, and Asia. In what ways could you increase your compassion for them? In what ways could you help others grow in compassion?

ILLUMINATIONS

When the heart grieves for what it has lost,
the soul rejoices for what it has found.
—*Sufi wisdom, traditional*

Look at the birds of the air: they neither sow nor reap nor gather into barns, and yet your heavenly father feeds them. Are you not of more value than they? And which of you by being anxious can add one cubit to his span of life? And why are you anxious about clothing? Consider the lilies of the field, how they grow; they neither toil nor spin; yet I tell you not even Solomon in all his glory was arrayed like one of these.
—*Matthew 6:26–29*

Ancient mother, we hear you calling. Awaken us to our planet's desperate need for peace.

—*Source unknown*

It was on dark nights of deep sleep
that I dreamed the most, sunk in the well,
and woke rested, if not beautiful,
filled with some other power.

—*Denise Levertov, English poet (1923–1998)*

In every danger, you can find a refuge in Mary.

—*St. Thomas Aquinas, theologian (1226–1274)*

The LORD your God is bringing you into a good land, a land of brooks and water, of fountains and springs, flowing forth in valleys and hills, a land of wheat and barley, of vines and fig trees and pomegranates, a land of olive trees and honey, a land in which you will eat bread without scarcity, in which you will lack nothing. . . . You will eat and have all you want and you shall bless the LORD your God for the good land he has given you.

—*Deuteronomy 8:7–9a, 10*

PRAYERS

TI PREGO[48]

This season, Lord,

I feel like the dogwood tree,

Twisted, wind-whipped,

Frost-stripped,

Because the thaw came too quickly, Lord,

Too early—

Then the freeze.

The blooms hurt, Lord.

Trying to bud again

With tips ice-burnt,

Brown-burnt

Trying to feel spring, Lord,

Trying to feel, Lord,

Wanting to feel the bloom again,

    But when?

When, Lord, when?

Amen[49]

—M.P.A. Schaeffer, *contemporary American poet*

If you protect me, Mary,
your divine son will receive me
into the company of the saints
who walk with him in paradise.
I am like a lost sheep
whose shepherd is searching for it;
seek me, mother of mercy.
Bring me safely home.[50]

—*Raissa Maritain, Russian contemplative (1883–1960)*

Hail Mary of the Third World, full of grace, you who know pain, know the anxieties and the subhuman conditions of your people, the Lord is with you, as with all who suffer, who are hungry and thirst for justice, who know neither letters nor numbers.

Blessed are you among women, the women and men of the roads and pueblos, of furrowed faces, of brawny muscles, of calloused hands, of forlorn eyes—but with hope.

Blessed is the fruit of your womb, Jesus. Because without him, our life and the struggle for human dignity has no meaning.

Holy Mary, all of you holy, you are a thousand times holy, by your life, by the times that you carry water, that you smudge your face at the hearth, trusting and hoping in God, who has made you alone the Mother of God.

Pray for us, because it is the fault of our human egoism and envy that you, united with all poor women and men, suffer misery, totalitarian governments, economic repression, wars and blood and hatred.

Pray for us now, so that we change, so that there will be a vast conversion of heart, and all women and men everywhere will turn towards Jesus, our brother, your son. And pray for us at the hour of our death, so that the Lord will have mercy on those who have offended him in their brothers and sisters, the men and women of a world that is struggling desperately for life. Amen.

—*Latin American oral tradition, written down by*
  Fr. Antonio Esquivel, SJ

FREEING THE CREATIVE SPIRIT

Make a list of things you would want to take with you if you were forced to leave home and move to a foreign country. Allow yourself only five minutes to complete the list, in order to gain a sense of Mary's dilemma when she, Joseph, and Jesus had to flee in the night for Egypt. Write the list as quickly as you can to be as thorough as possible. Pay attention to your thoughts and feelings when you write down specific items and realize how many treasured possessions must be left behind. Notice the memories of precious moments that come to mind. If you keep photograph albums, think of the difficulty of selecting only one album to carry with you and having to part with all the others. What clothes and medicines would you pack? What books and music would you carry with you? What food items? What would you miss the most?

The Holy Family owned few material possessions; nevertheless, leaving home entailed a staggering loss. Perhaps it would be worse for us who have so much.

When you have finished, go back over your list, reading it several times. Notice the kinds of items you included, as well as the kinds of things you had to exclude. Reflect on your choices. Do you find yourself wishing you could change your mind and rewrite the list? From this exercise, what have you learned about yourself and your relationship to your belongings?

FINDING
HER MISSING SON

Mary Finds Her Twelve-Year-Old Son
Debating with Learned Men
(Luke 2:41–51)

LISTENING TO SCRIPTURE

Jesus' parents went to Jerusalem every year at the feast of the Passover. And when he was twelve years old, they went up according to custom; and when the feast was ended, as they were returning, the boy Jesus stayed behind in Jerusalem. His parents did not know it, but supposing him to be in the company, they went a day's journey, and they sought him among their kinsfolk and acquaintances; and when they did not find him, they returned to Jerusalem, seeking him. After three days they found him in the temple, sitting among the teachers, listening to them and asking them questions; and all who heard him were amazed at his understanding and his answers. And when [Mary and Joseph] saw him they were astonished; and his mother said to him, "Son, why have you treated us so? Behold, your father and I have been looking for you anxiously." And he said to them, "How is it that you sought me? Did you not know that I must be in my Father's house?" And they did not understand the saying which he spoke to them. And he went down with them and came to Nazareth, and was obedient to them; and his mother kept all these things in her heart. (Luke 2:41–51)

IMAGINING THE STORY

It is a warm morning under a brilliant blue sky in spring of the year 13. Mary, Joseph, and their extended family are traveling home from Jerusalem with other Nazarene families after a joyful celebration of Passover rites and festivities. There are so many people, donkeys, and wooden carts piled high with provisions covered by billowing white cloths that Mary and Joseph's view of the full caravan is blocked. They are not aware that their twelve-year-old son is not with the group of boys who like to walk together.

In some ways, the scene resembles that of American pioneers in a covered-wagon train on the Oregon Trail in the nineteenth century. Jesus' family is too poor to own an ox, of course, and the ropes Joseph fashioned to strap down the wagon cover are made of reeds and rushes, rather than rawhide.

Imagine the scene. What do you see in the desert as Mary and Joseph make their way home? Scrub brush? A green valley? Water? Olive trees, date palms, other fruit trees, lily of the valley, roses, anemones? Is it a lonely landscape? What sounds can you hear?

The caravan stops to eat. Jesus is expected to join his parents, but fails to appear. Mary and Joseph call him, but receive no answer, and send a boy to tell Jesus his family is waiting for him. But the boy comes back alone. "He is not here," the boy replies. What do you imagine Mary and Joseph are feeling? They rush up and down both sides of the caravan, calling out his name—"Jesus! Jesus!"—over the din of happy voices talking, telling stories, singing, and laughing. It begins to dawn on Mary that her child cannot be found. One minute terrified, the next minute trying to trust, Mary hopes he and his friends are playing a joke, but soon realizes that he is truly missing.

Can you imagine the fountain of emotions welling up in Mary's soul? Anxiety? Panic? Frustration? Guilt? What would you be feeling in her place? Perhaps you have felt something similar when a child in your care cannot be found. Would you blame yourself for not knowing where your child is? What would you do? What would you be praying?

Mary and Joseph have no choice but to return to Jerusalem. An anguished day and a sleepless night filled with terror drag by before they reach the outskirts of the city, exhausted, wondering how they will find the strength to search the huge city. Public buildings and narrow streets still teem with pilgrims, soldiers, buyers and sellers, priests, women and children, plus the usual astrologers, snake charmers, wonder workers, and other charlatans who flock to the city at festival times.

The couple is almost beside themselves by the time they decide to begin with the temple. Jesus is so intent on religion and spirituality, so impassioned for God and learning, that he might have stayed in the temple, losing track of time. As they hurry toward the court of women where Joseph will have to leave Mary before he searches for Jesus, they suddenly hear voices enthusiastically discussing a theological point. Amazed, they recognize the sound of Jesus' voice, firm and clear, debating with the great scholars surrounding him.

Jesus, a boy on the verge of manhood, is oblivious to the pain he has caused his family. If you were Mary, what would you be feeling? What would you do? Picture her as she barges into the all-male group of scholars and interrupts their animated discussion with a rebuke directed at her son: "How could you do this to us!" Does it surprise you to see this side of Mary's character? Does it make her more interesting and real?

Jesus responds with a rebuke of his own: "Did you not know that I must be in my Father's house?" How do you imagine the look on Mary's face when her son speaks to her like this? Is she annoyed? Does she tell him to leave the discussion immediately and come with her? Is her heart bursting with pride and amazement at his spiritual and intellectual skill? Do you imagine her hugging her son and smiling with relief and delight that he is safe?

MEDITATIONS

Step 9 limns a whole new aspect of Mary's character that confirms she is growing from strength to strength. At twenty-five, with the rewards and challenges of motherhood mounting, she exhibits the fullness of feminine power through which she approaches daily challenges confidently and successfully. Entrusted with the formidable task of raising a divinely gifted and exceptional son, she has risen to the challenge with ever-increasing learning, insight, and love.

Understanding a boy on the brink of manhood is demanding enough, but there is no precedent for understanding a child whose whole being is absorbed spiritually, whose young passions are all directed toward God. Everything about Mary's son transcends human categories: what he says, his fervor for sacred Scripture, the long hours he devotes to studying Torah and saying prayers. When his mother confronts him in the temple with his thoughtlessness and the pain he has caused his family by not joining the caravan headed home, it is not surprising that his unapologetic reply is cryptic and deep: "Did you not know that I must be in my Father's house?"

What does Jesus mean by this puzzling question? Is it an adolescent's counter to a parental rebuke that brought an embarrassing end to his first scholarly disputation? Mary is too proud of her son to entertain such a negative interpretation. Perhaps the event marks an important milestone of coming of age in Jesus' life, the beginning of his self-understanding as the Son of God. Or perhaps he reveals for the first time in public the prodigy he and his mother always knew he was. What is clear is that at only twelve, Jesus can converse at the lofty level of highly learned men, asking and answering theological questions with the eloquence and authority of a Pharisee, although no Pharisee ever exhibited or encountered such gifts in one so young.

Step 9 on *The Way of Mary* has a vitally important teaching for us about everyday life in our homes. The story closes with the reunited family at home, and it is noted that Jesus "was obedient to his parents." This detail gives us a significant look into the home Mary has created in order to provide her child with a loving, supportive, nourishing foundation for life. We know nothing about his appearance, whether he was healthy or sickly, whether he played with neighborhood boys or preferred to go for walks alone in the hills. But we do know his parents instilled in Jesus a broad and deep love for learning that stayed with him all his life. The stories and parables he taught during his adult ministry reveal enormous learning and reflection in many fields of knowledge, ranging from religion and philosophy to politics and economics. It is not surprising that the adult Jesus would prefer Mary of Bethany's[51] way of contemplating and learning from his teachings over Martha's way of busying herself and becoming distracted. (See Luke 10:38–42.)

Jesus also received a solid and extensive religious foundation in his home that saturated his soul with Mary and Joseph's contagious love for prayer and learning the Scriptures. As the story for Step 9 suggests, Jesus' obligation to be obedient to his parents (Luke 2:51) relates to the fourth commandment to honor one's father and mother. Obviously, Mary taught her son to observe all of the Ten Commandments, especially keeping the Sabbath holy. There were more than six hundred sacred duties of Jewish religious life to be learned and observed, and pilgrimages had to be made to Jerusalem annually for Passover rites. Daily prayers were said, and blessings for countless aspects of everyday life were prayed.

Whether we ourselves live in a family, with friends, alone, or in a community, there is no limit to the joy of life and moments of grace attainable by creating, as Mary did, an atmosphere in the home permeated by the love of learning and spiritual practice.

Jesus' debut in the temple gave Mary yet another profound experience to ponder in her heart and treasure in her memory, each a thread dropped by God on her path. One can dismiss and walk by such a thread, or stop to pick it up and explore it for hidden colors, connections, and contrasts that fit the design of one's life. For those who stop, it is as though every thread is imprinted with direction and divinity, and to gather these threads together is to create an original and beautiful work of art.

In a book with a lovely title, *Purity of Heart Is to Will One Thing*, the Lutheran philosopher Søren Kierkegaard wrote a passage that could be called "The Spirituality of Sewing" (or knitting, crocheting, quilting, or similar work).[52] Describing a woman who is making an altar cloth, he says, "She withholds nothing." She gives her all in every stitch; it is her "highest happiness," and she loses herself in the task because she loves it, and accomplishes it for God. Similarly, with each thread of deep experience we consciously sew into our life story, we become more focused and present in the moment while moving a little closer to the distant horizon of our life and the beautiful pattern of individuality and personhood we take to God.

Mysteriously and incomprehensibly, a dozen years before this event in the temple, Spirit changed into a human baby in Mary's womb. Every year since then, she grew in insight and understanding of her son and, as always when we seek to truly understand another person, the rewards were incalculable. Every such effort brings us closer, not only to the other person's spirit, but to our own. And that is the place from which we are capable of real love.

REFLECTION QUESTIONS

- Do you look for threads dropped on your path? When did you most recently find one of these threads? Did it teach you something about the direction you were following? When did you ignore a thread God placed before you?

- Some people think that Jesus' response to his mother implies a rebuke: "You ought to have known I was in the temple!" How do you understand his response?

- Some people think that in adulthood Jesus was a Pharisee. Among their reasons are the eloquence of his speech, the breadth and depth of his learning (Luke 4:16–20; John 8:1–11), and his highly developed intelligence and wisdom. What is your opinion about this? Does it matter whether or not he was a Pharisee?

- Today people all over the world report visions of Mary and often say they hear her urging us to pray for peace. Do you consider these visions helpful for humanity?

ILLUMINATIONS

> In that little town, my son, where they knew us together,
> you called me mother; but no one had eyes to see
> the astounding events as they took place day by day.
> Your life became the life of the poor
> in your wish to be with them through the work of your
>   hands.
>
> I knew: the light that lingered in ordinary things,
> like a spark sheltered under the skin of our days—
> the light was you;
> it did not come from me.
>
> And I had more of you in that luminous silence
> than I had of you as the fruit of my body, my blood.[53]
> —*Pope John Paul II, from "The Mother"*

> I do not wish for anything you can give me, oh my sweet
> love, but only for you.[54]
>
> —*St. Catherine of Genoa, writer and activist (1447–1510)*

The loss of her child surpassed for Mary the loss of anything in creation, for her love and appreciation of him exceeded anything she could conceive of. She knew, she trusted that angels were with her, but they did not help her know where her child was. The blessings and consolations from God that this great soul so often received were not given. There was no relief to her pain.[55]

—*Mary of Agreda, Spanish visionary (1502–1665)*

You would not seek if you had not already found.[56]

—*Blaise Pascal, French geometrician (1623–1662)*

PRAYERS

The LORD is my shepherd.

I shall not want.

He makes me to lie down in green pastures.

He restores my soul

He guides me

in paths of saving justice

for his name's sake.

Even though I walk through the valley of the shadow of death,

I fear no evil;

for you are with me;

your staff is there

to comfort me.

You prepare a table before me

in the presence of my enemies;

you anoint my head with oil,

my cup overflows.

Surely goodness and kindness will follow me
all the days of my life;
and I will dwell in the house of the LORD forever.
—*Psalm 23:1–6*

Star of this stormy sea . . .
Turn your heart to the terrifying squall
in which I find myself,
alone,
without a map.[57]
—*Petrarch (Francesco Petrarca), Italian humanist (1304–1374)*

O Mary, intercede for the children. There are too many missing children; too many desperate children orphaned in war; children made homeless by wild storms, droughts, and famines; hopeless children trapped in refugee camps; babies born addicted or HIV positive. Help us to understand that the injustice these little ones suffer is human-caused.

Hear our prayer to heal those who are indifferent: social structures, institutions, and leaders who rule with swollen egos and empty hearts. Pray for us, Mary, to not rest until every child is nourished, healed, and freed from soul-warping hands. O Mary, intercede for the children. Ask with us for every infant to grow up loved. Help us to intercede so that their eyes shine with love instead of tears. Give us the grace to undo what the world has done.

—*Source unknown*

FREEING THE CREATIVE SPIRIT

Review the Freeing the Creative Spirit section in Step 5, page 103 above. In that exercise, you were given a set of alternative mysteries for saying the Rosary that were called the Rites of Passage Mysteries. You were guided to choose five "rites of passage" from your own life and to then meditate on these personal mysteries while saying the Rosary.

To practice freeing the creative spirit today, create an entirely new set of mysteries to ponder while praying the Rosary—not another set of Rites of Passage Mysteries but, instead, your own unique category. For example, you might choose "the Sacramental Mysteries." If you have received five sacraments, for instance, baptism, reconciliation, the Eucharist, confirmation, and marriage, you could meditate on one sacrament with each decade.

If nothing comes immediately to your mind, try asking yourself what five persons, biblical passages, global issues, problems, or blessings you would like to ruminate on. They must be suitable for prayerful reflection, of course. Look back over your life or around the world for ideas. Walking through the rooms in your home might generate ideas. Consider what is on your schedule today and what is in the news. Try sitting still for a few minutes to turn inside and wait for ideas to surface in the silence.

Give your imagination free rein, and after you have shaped your first set of alternative mysteries, pray the Rosary with them.

When you are ready, begin fashioning yet another group of sacred mysteries. There is almost no end to the possibilities.

THE WEDDING AT CANA

*Mary Intervenes to Help Inaugurate
Her Son's Public Ministry* (John 2:1–11)

LISTENING TO SCRIPTURE

*There was a wedding at Cana in Galilee. The mother of Jesus
was there, and Jesus and his disciples had also been invited. And
they ran out of wine, since the wine provided for the feast had all
been used, and the mother of Jesus said to him, "They have no
wine." Jesus said to her, "Woman, what do you want from me?
My hour has not come yet." His mother said to the servants, "Do
whatever he tells you." There were six stone jars standing there,
meant for the ablutions that are customary among the Jews: each
could hold twenty or thirty gallons. Jesus said to the servants: "Fill
the jars with water," and they filled them to the brim. Then he
said to them, "Draw some out now and take it to the president of
the feast." They did this; the president tasted the water, and it had
turned into wine. Having no idea where it came from—though
the servants who had drawn the water knew—the president of the
feast called the bridegroom and said, "Everyone serves the good
wine first and the worse wine when the guests are well wined;
but you have kept the best wine until now."*

*This was the first of Jesus' signs; it was at Cana in Galilee. He
revealed his glory, and his disciples believed in him. (John 2:1–11)*

IMAGINING THE STORY

It is the year we call 30, and a gala wedding is underway in Cana, a village three miles from Mary's home in Nazareth. According to custom, the wedding party continues for seven days, with some guests remaining all week and others arriving throughout the week. Men and women come and go, festively dressed in special clothes reserved for weddings. Mary, perhaps a relative of the newly married couple, is talking and laughing with friends while Jesus and his small group of disciples enjoy a spirited discussion while drinking and eating on the other side of the room. Pungent aromas of roast lamb and spices mingle with the sweet fragrances of roses, anemones, and lilies.

In your imagination, picture the scene. Is the party in a private home? What do you see as you look around? Is there music and dancing? How do the guests' wedding garments differ from the homespun tunics and sandals worn during the week? Can you see the six big stone jars that will soon take on unforgettable significance? Each holds from fifteen to twenty-five gallons of water.

Imagine that Mary overhears the head server whisper to the groom that the wine has run out. What is the groom's facial expression? What is he feeling? Does he tell the bride? Watch as Mary goes over to Jesus to tell him there is no more wine, then instructs the servers to do whatever Jesus tells them. Are you surprised by the way Mary takes charge? Does this assertiveness change your image of her?

Suddenly, the music and dancing stop, and exclamations of wonder and amazement are heard all over the room. Everyone is asking what happened. How is it possible that in the presence of a hundred reliable witnesses, water has turned into wine? What is your response? Are people shocked that a mere woodworker from Nazareth can achieve such a great feat?

As the servers distribute the new wine, imagine yourself moving close to Mary so you can speak to her from your heart. Would you like to express admiration for what she did today? Would you like to talk about Jesus' spiritual powers?

MEDITATIONS

Now in her early forties, Mary appears in full flowering as a mature, self-confident, wise, and effective woman who is blessed with deep prophetic insight. At a wedding feast, a surprising event takes place that reveals the depth and breadth of her character and capabilities in this new era of her life. It is toward the end of the week-long festivities when a server whispers to the hosts that the wine has run out. Mary realizes this will be an emotional catastrophe for the young bride and groom, unforgettably embarrassing for their parents and grandparents, ruining both families' memories of the wedding. Meat and sweets are plentiful, as are cake and red grapes, figs and dates, but without wine, the celebration is sure to end days earlier than planned. Mary knows that Jesus can save the situation if, at first, *she* intervenes.

Once again, as on the first day of our pilgrimage with Mary, she is confronted with a choice. She can urge Jesus to use powers that only she knows he has, or she can step aside from the young couple's predicament, remaining uninvolved as though she does not care or is powerless to help. If she intercedes and Jesus does what she knows he can do, this will set his public ministry into motion, compelling him to reveal his real identity on a schedule other than his own. Apparently God wants Mary to help inaugurate Jesus' ministry.

Like great prophets before her, Mary sees intuitively that a providential moment has arrived. It is time for the world to learn who Jesus is. It is time for his divine powers to be publicly revealed, and it is she who can help him carry out God's will. She would like to encourage him, just as she nudged him to take steps when he was learning to walk. Often it was she who pointed the way when he was a boy. On the other hand, he is thirty now, no longer young, perhaps less susceptible to maternal interference.

Mary makes a choice. She goes over to Jesus and whispers that the wine has run out, implicitly asking him to solve the problem. Jesus protests that the situation has nothing to do with him—or with her, for that matter—apparently refusing to get involved. But Mary acts as though he had agreed and instructs the servers to do whatever he tells them.

And Jesus does what his mother knew he could do: he performs his first sign, his first miracle. He turns ordinary well water into delicious wine, and in the process turns the entire world inside out. He changes no less than the whole relationship between God and humankind, replacing the old covenant in law with the new covenant in love. Through her first act of intercession, Mary helps Jesus to begin the work that will end in his death three years later.

As the doorway through which her son entered life, she is now the doorway through which he re-enters life, this time disclosed in his full personhood as the Anointed One of God.

This powerful and beautiful story ends on a note of breathtaking wonder and gladness for Mary, and with wonderful implications for ourselves. Just as she helps her son come into his own, so she can help us find our true identity and the work that best fits our soul. Just as she intervenes for the bride and groom at Cana, so she can help us change whatever needs to be changed. We need only recall her guidance, "Do whatever he tells you." Seek and follow the infinite wisdom of her son. As Christians, we have the unimaginably precious legacy of his teachings in our hearts and communities, and this legacy tells us all we need to know to be in the most joyful, rewarding place one can be: aligned with God's desires for our lives. Also as Christians, we have a mother to turn to for the grace of carrying out whatever we must do.

We need to remember how decisively, how graciously, Mary takes charge at Cana; how far and wide this one small action and these few words ripple across space and time; how love alone inspires her. May we be aware that the power of her intercession lies as close as our fingertips, and that she always responds to prayer.

REFLECTION QUESTIONS

- On two occasions, Mary is a doorway through which Jesus enters the world: first as a newborn baby boy, and second as the Anointed One of God. What door would you like her to open for you?

- Mary's *belief* that an exhausted supply of wine could flow again sets the great events at Cana into motion. Do you, too, believe that scarcity can turn into abundance (whether spiritual things—such as joy, courage, forgiveness, and love; or material things—such as housing, education, financial security)? What experience of yours exemplifies scarcity turning into abundance?

- At Cana, Mary's intercessory role led to Jesus' first miracle, an event that illustrates the remarkable power in her interventions. Have you asked her to intervene for you? If so, what experience of yours illustrates how she can concretely help?

- Since Mary has a mediating role between God and all of God's people, do you ask her to intercede in the lives of your friends and family, as well as in global situations? Is there someone in particular for whom you would like to invite her intercession? Is there a particular global situation?

- A number of theologians have remarked that Jesus *is* the center of Christianity, and Mary is *at* the center. Notice that Mary always guides people toward Jesus, not to herself, as at Cana when she tells the servers to do whatever Jesus says. Why is that important?

ILLUMINATIONS

When a great moment knocks on the door of your life, it is often no louder than the beating of your heart; and it is very easy to miss.[58]

—*Boris Pasternak, Russian novelist (1890–1960)*

Now is the acceptable time.

—*2 Corinthians 6:2b*

For everything there is a season,
 and a time for every matter under heaven:
A time to be born, and a time to die;
A time to plant, and a time to reap;
A time to kill, and a time to heal;
A time to break down, and a time to build up;
A time to weep, and a time to laugh;
A time to mourn, and a time to dance;

—*Ecclesiastes 3:1–5*

O Mary, you were promised in Eden as the woman who would right Eve's wrongs, the woman whose child would crush the serpent's head. Help us to conquer the evil that surrounds us everywhere, the physical, mental, moral, and environmental toxins that infect our homes and hearts, our workplaces and institutions. With the grace of your son, Jesus Christ, we can overcome these evil poisons through the vastness of your love.

O Mary, mother of Jesus the prince of peace, convert by his divine power, which surpasses all human power, the enemies of peace who ruin lives and destroy everything that is good. Bring to justice the dictators and tyrants and autocrats who illegally run dozens of the world's countries, daring to decide who lives or dies, who prospers or starves, who is jailed or goes free, as though they were themselves the God who created us all.

O Mary, win our hearts with your beauty so that we who want to do good in the family, community, and world will follow your way of faith and love, and be drawn to all the teachings of your son, especially his guidance to seek spiritual understanding before we speak or act. Conquer in us—and help us to conquer in ourselves—whatever resistance, inertia, or distractions block our good intentions.

Holy Mary *Conquistadora,* beloved mother of us all, we pray in deep gratitude for knowing you as a "conqueror," a woman of strength and courage who dares to take bold initiatives in the service of God's purposes. We honor you in this life with all our hearts and minds and will embrace you in the next, forever with all the saints, through the grace of your divine son, Jesus Christ, our Lord.

—*Anonymous twentieth-century prayer from Latin America*

Ave Regina,[59]
holy, loving,
most noble queen.
Ave Maris Stella,
star of the sea and
moon where God took hiding.
But for you,
holy mother of God,
would the world have been lost.

—*From an anonymous fourteenth-century penitential song*

FREEING THE CREATIVE SPIRIT

Think back to Mary's great psalm of praise in Step 3, the Magnificat, which opens with the words, "My soul magnifies the Lord, and my spirit rejoices in God my Savior" (Luke 1:46), and create your own expression of praise and gratitude to God. Begin by choosing the form, the medium of artistic expression that you are most comfortable with, whether or not you consider yourself talented in that medium. It is absolutely essential to know that no gift, ability, or talent is required to perform this practice with great success and joy! It might even be wise to settle on a medium you have never tried before now. People often make fascinating discoveries when they try to draw with the nondominant hand—that is, a right-handed person draws with the left hand, and vice versa.

This practice of freeing the creative spirit offers an opportunity for newness that you may wish to try. There is no obligation to do so, of course, especially if the very thought of taking on something unfamiliar gives you a shiver of anxiety.

Here are some forms of expression that you may wish to choose from:

You could try your hand at writing—for example, a poem, a song, or a prayer. If you have time for a substantial undertaking, you could write a play. It is fine to compose with a pen or pencil on paper or to use a computer.

If you enjoy dancing, then let yourself move to the unique rhythm of your heart, swaying, leaping, turning, jumping for joy. Move as slowly or rapidly as feels right:

close to the floor, or stretching tall; sweeping through all the rooms in your home, or remaining in a circumscribed space. Play music you love in the background, or sing, or allow your body movements to take you deeper and deeper into silence. Please remember that the less gifted you think you are in the selected form of expression, the more freely you may be able to create your psalm of praise. You will stay focused in the present moment with fewer concerns about the outcome and quality of your work.

Perhaps you would like to draw or paint your expression of praise. Colored pens and pencils, markers, crayons, watercolors, and oils are all fine. For a sculpture, wire or children's clay is more than adequate. For a collage, your home will supply in abundance all the materials you need. Wonderful artwork can also be accomplished on a computer, and many people like to burn a CD containing their creations. For the more ambitious who might like to make a film, a home video camera and a liberated imagination suffice.

There is also the possibility of making a recording. If you opt for a recording, you can find right in your own home a wonderful array of beautiful sounds to include, such as your own voice speaking, praying, reading a passage from a book you love, chanting, humming, or singing. If you know how to sing in harmony, you could create a voiceover. First, record yourself singing a song, then re-record the same song while harmonizing with your own voice. The results will delight you.

If you would like to hear the uplifting sound of a waterfall in the background, try placing different kinds of materials in the sink where the tap water falls until you have the sound you are looking for. A plastic cutting board will give a different result from a wooden cutting board or crinkled tinfoil. (Please be sure to recycle the water used, out of concern for the planet's shortages.)

Select the medium in which to create, gather any materials you will need, and you are ready to start your psalm of praise. Begin by bringing to mind the beautiful opening words of the Magnificat, "My soul magnifies the Lord." Think about the enormity and power implicit in that statement. Today it is *your* soul that magnifies, increases, and enlarges the Holy Presence in the world. Repeat those five charged words several times, aloud if you like: *My—soul—magnifies—the—Lord*, until you feel new energy rising inside. Now let your soul take flight. Write, sing, dance, draw, build, create your praise and gratitude for the great things God has done for you.

Continue as you wish. The size or length of your sacred project is up to you. If you are so inclined, you may want to make this a major work that you execute over time.

AT THE CROSS

Mary Stands at the Foot of the Cross
with Her Sister,
the Beloved Disciple John,
and Mary Magdalene
(John 19:25)

LISTENING TO SCRIPTURE

Standing by the cross of Jesus were his mother, and his mother's
sister, Mary the wife of Clopas, and Mary Magdalene.
(John 19:25)

IMAGINING THE STORY

It is mid-afternoon on a Friday in about the year 33, and
the springtime sky has grown ominously dark, as though
a devastating storm is threatening. A handful of people are
gathered on the stony hill of Golgotha where criminals
are frequently executed. But today an innocent man is
being killed.

Several hours ago, the Roman authority in Galilee,
Pontius Pilate, released from prison a highly prominent
and popular young revolutionary named Barabbas who
had been condemned to death for leading an insurrection
against the Roman occupiers. In exchange for Barabbas,

Pilate sentenced Mary's son, Jesus, a comparatively unknown leader of a small Jewish religious movement, to be crucified—an unspeakably cruel means of capital punishment intended to inflict maximum suffering. Jesus' small band of followers have fled in all directions in fear for their own lives.

Only four loyal people remain with the dying Christ at the foot of the cross: his mother and three of the closest disciples—Mary, the wife of Clopas; John, the beloved disciple; and a woman who is special to Jesus, Mary Magdalene. These few faithful people walked the way of the cross with Jesus and for almost three excruciating hours have stood by while the person they love most in the world is slowly dying a horrific, barbaric death.

Can you imagine yourself there on the grim hill of Golgotha with a handful of Roman soldiers, Mary, the three anguished disciples, and the dying Son of God? What would that be like for you? What would you be feeling? What would you want to do? How would you persuade yourself to remain until the end? Would you be praying? What would you pray?

Look briefly at Mary. How would you describe her suffering? How do you respond to her pain? Is there anything you can say or do to comfort her? Do you prefer to wait and be with her in silence? What do you pray?

MEDITATIONS

No one has been more often portrayed in art than Mary to illustrate the heights and depths of joy and sorrow; no picture of sorrow has made a deeper impression on the human soul than Mary in the presence of her dying son. Powerless to protect him, longing to shriek at the soldiers, "Leave him alone! Take *me*!" but unable to die in his place, she stands at his side while his body is drained of all human strength, drop by drop. Mary, the mother of the God-man she believed to be the hope of the world, is pushed toward the breaking point by overwhelming anguish and exhaustion.

Michelangelo's magnificent *Pietà* draws millions of pilgrims each year to St. Peter's Basilica in Rome to experience the paradoxical pain and beauty of grief carved into radiant, white marble. Unspeakably moving, this sculpture radiates with the holiness of the eternal minute after Jesus is taken down from the cross, and his mother holds her dead son in her lap. The divine tragedy could not be envisioned more humanly or exquisitely than in this culminating scene that brings an end to Jesus' suffering, while Mary's goes on. She is left behind, alone and desolate, without hope of any kind, faith suspended in the sheer magnitude of the void. One thinks of the poet Rainer Maria Rilke's words:

> O shooting star
> that fell into my eyes and through my body:
> Not to forget you. To endure.[60]

All over the world and across time, grieving men and women have turned for comfort and strength to Mary, the beloved mother who more than any woman in human memory exemplifies a way of suffering that enables us in our own sorrow to believe that we, too, can endure and go on. Since the earliest Christian centuries, believers have turned to Mary in times of suffering because the Christian God is a crucified God, and she is his mother, the mother of sorrow who underwent his ordeal vicariously, as any loving mother would. At the foot of a cross that ever since has symbolized ultimate human suffering, she watched and listened and felt him die in her heart.

A mother's suffering when her child suffers is indescribable. Mary is closer to Jesus than anyone else on earth. His face resembles hers; his words and gestures resemble hers; even his stories and parables reflect her influence. She is the only person to ever be fully informed about the Christ, the one who knows him more intimately than anyone else, and the one who lost the most when he died.

Mary experienced what mothers of suffering and dying children all over the world endure every day, and they turn to her by the millions for the courage to stand firm in the working out of God's will. As she once stood at the foot of the cross, she stands with poor mothers who are powerless to save children from hunger; with wealthy mothers of children ravaged by disease; with single mothers who cannot make ends meet; with mothers of the "disappeared," the young who vanish by the thousands in Latin America, Asia, Africa, and the Middle East for resisting, protesting, and questioning corrupt authority—as Jesus did.

The staggering turn of events on that dark Friday afternoon—the unfathomable murder of God—brings to a brutal and sudden end all the dreams and visions and hopes that Jesus set on fire in his followers' hearts. Souls split apart as their world becomes a pile of dust. Were they all duped by Jesus' magnificent teaching and preaching and miraculous signs? These must have been the thoughts in many hearts after such a bitter, unjust slaughter of an innocent, holy man. Surely no one—not even Mary—could remember in such sorrow Jesus' distant promises to rise on the third day, revivified, restored, reborn.

But precisely three days after his death, Jesus returned in his resurrected body, giving his mother and other disciples and all humankind the sacred teaching and assurance that we, too, will live after death. As the Gospels record: "Blessed are you who weep now, for you will laugh" (Luke 6:21b).

REFLECTION QUESTIONS

- The Christian God is a God who suffers, and Mary his mother suffers with him. Does this help you to acknowledge and understand your own suffering? What methods do you use to express your suffering—prayer, pondering, telling a trusted person, journaling, expressing through art, protest?

- Many people turn to Mary in times of suffering. Some ask her for comfort and strength. Others ask her for the grace of dignity or endurance or spiritual growth during difficult times. Can you think of a difficult time in your own life when you were able to pray despite the pain? Did you pray to Mary? If so, what did you ask her?

- Intercessory prayer, prayer for others, is one of the most beautiful and spiritually beneficial forms of prayer. Not only are we ourselves helped by praying for others, but also our prayers genuinely help them (as in the case of hospital patients who heal more quickly when prayed for). Think of a time when you were prayed for by others. How did it help?

- The most powerful and effective form of intercessory prayer is Mary's. Only her son's compassion is greater than hers. Do you strive to imitate her compassion? Do you ask her to intercede with her son for yourself, for loved ones, or for world problems? How do you feel when you ask her to intercede?

ILLUMINATIONS

Mama,

why have you come?

You cause me a mortal wound,

for your weeping pierces me

like the sharpest sword.

Son, pale and ruddy,

Son, without compare:

Son, on whom will I rely?

Son, why are you abandoning me?

Son, pale and white,

Son of the laughing face,

Son, why has the world,

O my son, so hated you?[61]

—*Jacopone da Todi, Franciscan mystic and poet (ca 1230–1306)*

Can you hear me? I would like to fling my voice out like a
     cloth

over the fragments of your death, and keep pulling at it until
     it is

torn to pieces, and all my words would have to walk around

shivering, in the tatters of that voice: if lament were

     enough.[62]

—*Rainer Maria Rilke*

Even in the midst of great pain, Lord,
I praise You for that which is. . . .
I pray for whatever you send me,
and I ask to receive it as your gift.[63]
—*From Psalm 4, version of the poet Stephen Mitchell*

. . . He did not cling
to his equality with God
but emptied himself
to assume the condition of a slave,
and became as men are;
he was humbler yet,
even to accepting death,
death on a cross.
—*Philippians 2:6–11*

I am with you always.
—*Matthew 28:20b*

We hope you will enjoy this book and find it useful in enriching your life.

Book title:

Your comments:

How you learned about this book:

Reasons why you bought this book: *(check all that apply)*

☐ Subject   ☐ Author   ☐ Attractive Cover   ☐ Attractive Inside

☐ Recommendation of Friend   ☐ Recommendation of Reviewer   ☐ Gift

If purchased: Bookseller _____ City _____ State _____

Please send me information about: *(check all that apply)*

1. ☐ Spirituality   4. ☐ Fiction   6. ☐ Other _____
2. ☐ Theology   5. ☐ Religious Traditions (Which ones?)
3. ☐ Prayer/Worship   _____

Name (PRINT) _____ Phone _____

Street _____ City _____ State _____ Zip _____

E-mail _____

PARACLETE PRESS

PARACLETE PRESS

PO Box 1568

Orleans, MA 02653

PRAYERS

LAMENT OF MARY

> I am overwhelmed, O my son,
>
> I am overwhelmed by love
>
> And I cannot endure
>
> that I should be in the chamber
>
> and you on the wood of the cross,
>
> I in the house
>
> and you in the tomb.[64]

—*St. Romanus Melodos, Syrian hymn writer first half of sixth century*

THERE IS A BROKENNESS

There is a brokenness
out of which comes the unbroken,
a shatteredness out
of which blooms the unshatterable.
There is a sorrow
beyond all grief which leads to joy
and a fragility
out of whose depths emerges strength.

There is a hollow space
too vast for words
through which we pass with each loss,
out of whose darkness
we are sanctioned into being.

There is a cry deeper than all sound
whose serrated edges cut the heart
as we break open
to the place inside which is unbreakable
and whole,
while learning to sing.[65]

—*Rashani, contemporary hermit*

Hail Mary, full of grace, the Lord is with you. Hail, hope of the needy, mother of those who no longer have a mother. O Mary, when my heart is full of grief, when my soul is enveloped in sadness and fear, when emotions storm inside me, when it seems that the gates of heaven have closed against me and robbed me of my relationship with God, to whom could I turn in my anguish but to you? O blessed Mary, consoler of the afflicted and refuge of sinners.[66]

—*Thomas à Kempis, German (1380–1471)*

FREEING THE CREATIVE SPIRIT

This exercise invites you to try a practice that will never be complete. It entails mapping the course of your Christian journey on a tree of Jesse. It is a clear and enjoyable method to discern the pattern of God's activity in one's life. The figure of the Jesse tree comes from the prophet Isaiah:

> There shall come forth a shoot
> From the stump of Jesse,
> And a branch shall grow out of his roots. (Isaiah 11:1)

Many Christians interpret the green "shoot" and "branch" that sprout from the apparently dead tree as symbols of Mary's and Jesus' births into the line of David, from which the Messiah was to come.

You will need a pencil and a plain white piece of paper, standard U.S. letter size or metric A4 size. Sketch a simple tree trunk by making two parallel, vertical lines, more or less at the center of the page. These two sides of your tree should be about an inch (25 mm.) apart and about three inches (75 mm.) tall, leaving sufficient space blank above and below the trunk to gradually fill in the root system and the branches.

Think about all the factors and influences that went into the building of your roots: your parents, for example, plus all the generations of ancestors; their religion and spirituality; their ethnicity; their language; their hard work; their education for a trade or profession; their genetic elements, positive and negative; and many more factors that will come to mind as you free your creative spirit. Becoming aware of your root system is to learn what is given and inalterable, like the color of your eyes. It is part of your grounding in the rich and fertile soil of the earth, the material you have to work with in the deeply spiritual process of becoming the person you are meant to become and finding the work you are meant to do. The foundation has been given; the building is up to you.

To begin charting your pilgrimage, draw a line downward or outward from the base of the tree trunk to represent one of your roots. Then write along it in small letters what it represents, for example Mom or Dad. The lines can be as straight, wavy, short, or long as you like, but be sure to leave room to fill in a great number of them as they come to you, little by little, over the course of time. Now draw another root and label it. Perhaps it stands for a beloved grandparent or uncle. Sketch and label another, then a fourth, and a fifth; keep going, as long as you wish.

Now draw a branch reaching upward or sideways, again using a simple line, in the crown section of the tree to represent the first step of your journey, and label it with a word or two. You may want to begin with baptism. Then ask yourself, for example, when and how you became conscious of yourself, of your identity as a Christian, and draw a branch to represent that. At what age did you first decide to live according to Christian values? That would make a good branch. Note influences such as a sacrament, a beloved member of the clergy, attending church with your family, or perhaps feeling intense love for God while praying. Draw a branch for each influence, person, or event that you recall. What was the next step in your pilgrimage? Draw a branch and label it. What losses or illnesses brought you closer to God? When did Mary enter your heart? Continue filling in branches and note on each what it stands for. If you went to a Christian school or a Sunday school, what kind of a role did that play in your spiritual development? When did you undergo a period of doubt?

Continue adding branches for a few minutes, and then begin drawing twigs that have grown out of the major branches—unpredictable offshoots of other events.

When you have at least a dozen roots, a dozen branches, and about the same number of twigs, spend some time looking for patterns. Can you see how the roots in which you are grounded gave you a good start in life? Did your appreciation of goodness, beauty, and truth begin in the family? Were your loftiest values there at your origins, handed down from the previous generation? Continue asking yourself questions like these to better understand the precious gifts transmitted to us all by our ancestors.

Concentrate on the crown section of the tree for a few minutes; then look at the tree as a whole. What patterns or meanings do you discern? Can you see how your relationship with Mary has evolved? Can you see how God has brought you to where you are now? Look for connections between roots and branches. Where do you notice good results coming out of misfortunes? Do you see the pattern of your calling unfolding?

Before closing the practice, look for direction pointers, patterns that suggest alternatives and choices. The future of your spiritual path is unknowable, but your decisions make all the difference. As many people have observed, when we look back on our journey, we can see why things happened, how one thing led to another, and how everything connects. But when we look forward, absolutely nothing is predictable. Decisions must be made every day. It is wise to be close to Mary when you make them.

JESUS SPEAKS TO MARY FROM THE CROSS

Mary Becomes the Spiritual Mother
of All Disciples for All Time
(John 19:26–27)

LISTENING TO SCRIPTURE

Seeing his mother and the disciple whom he loved standing near her, Jesus said to his mother, "Woman, this is your son." Then to the disciple he said, "This is your mother." And from that hour the disciple took her to his home. (John 19:26–27)

IMAGING THE STORY

For close to three hours, four anguished women and men have been keeping a deathwatch on the infamous hill of Golgotha under a heavy sky. They are the most loyal disciples of the holiest man who has ever lived, and they are crushed in mind and soul and spirit: his widowed mother, Mary; his most beloved woman friend, Mary Magdalene; the beloved disciple, John; and Mary, whose husband, Clopas, has fled with all the men, apostles and disciples, afraid of being arrested as accessories to Jesus' alleged crimes.

In ultimate contrast to the four great souls who would stand at the foot of the cross until the end of time if Jesus needed them there, several hateful Roman soldiers loll on the ground, playing dice as though they were bored. Soulless and indifferent to the suffering of the human being they nailed down three hours ago like carpenters making a fence, they may someday be spiritually awakened by the very men who have gone into hiding today. Those men are struggling to understand the divine tragedy that is underway on this "good" Friday afternoon, and in a few months they will be able to preach the gospel of love and reconciliation to the entire world.

Now Joseph of Arimathea arrives, determined that the sacred body will be taken down from the cross and given religious burial in a new tomb he recently purchased for himself. If he fails to obtain the body, whether by persuasion or other means, Jesus will be left on the cross indefinitely, like all victims of crucifixion, as a supposed deterrent to would-be criminals.

In your imagination, picture yourself near Mary and John at this time, as one of the most moving events in the Christian story occurs. How would you describe the way Mary appears? And John, who is some thirty years younger than she—how would you describe his appearance? The moment of Jesus' death is not far away, yet Jesus looks down from the cross at his mother and his beloved friend, and tells Mary that she is now John's mother; then he tells John that he is now Mary's son. How do they respond? With words? With body language?

MEDITATIONS

In this magnificent story from the divine drama playing out through Jesus and his mother, the tenderest love imaginable blends with the profoundest pain. Mary's dying son looks down from the cross, forcing himself to see into his mother's eyes one last time, absorbing the depth of her suffering, pulling himself together despite horrific suffering to focus on her and concentrate all his love, with all its vastness and tenderness and endlessness, to say goodbye. It is the hardest part of losing a loved one, this essential final physical separation and severing of precious ties.

Mary stands with John close beside her at the foot of the cross, their arms around each other now as they realize the excruciating deathwatch is drawing to a close. Jesus leans to speak to them, musters what little physical strength is left to put into words one of his greatest teachings, a teaching that will redirect history and transfigure humankind. What he wants before he dies is to make final and formal something that is already taking place between Mary and John: they are loving one another as Jesus has loved them (John 13:34b). A new spiritual reality is entering their support and care for one another, and Jesus wants to assure us that this sacred love will continue in the community he is birthing as he dies.

The teaching is simple and unforgettable. Jesus tells his mother that she is now the mother of John, and he tells John that he is now Mary's son. In other words, right at the height of divine and human grief, something new and wonderful is happening: Mary and John become spiritual relatives. They become mother and child, family members in the only community of forgiveness and love, which will sweep across the earth inviting each of us to begin again in a life of dignity and integrity. By bringing his beloved mother and his most beloved follower into a unique relationship that never existed before, bequeathing them a new way of relating, a way to connect in goodness and in enduring love, Jesus takes leave of the world with his divine Father's plan fulfilled.

This sacred parting of mother and son recalls a beautiful story from Vietnam told by Thich Nhat Hanh, or Thay, which has implications for all of us. Thay explained that he had a friend who had not seen her son for nearly twenty years.

> She told me that every time she misses her son, all she has to do is look at her hand and she feels better. Before he left, he held her hand and told her, "Whenever you miss me, look into your hand. You will see me immediately." For nearly 20 years, she has looked into her hands often. The presence of her son is not just genetic. His spirit, his hopes, and his life are also present to her. I hope that my friend practices meditation, because this subject, "Looking into your hand," can take her far in her spiritual practice. From the hand, she can penetrate deeply into reality. She will see that thousands of generations before her and thousands of generations after her are all she. From time immemorial until the present moment, her life has never

been interrupted and her hand is still there, a beginningless and endless reality.[67]

Because of Jesus' tender and poignant farewell gift from the cross two thousand years ago, we who are followers of Christ are bonded to one another at the depths of the soul. We have everything we need to love, to hold one another up, and to catch one another when we fall. Let us remind and inspire each other to invoke Mary, to ask her to mother the Christ in ourselves just as she mothered Jesus on earth, and to nurture our community just as she nourished the newborn community in the weeks and months and years after Jesus died and rose out of her physical sight.

Essential to Mary's universal motherhood is her availability in our time and always to raise children in the image of her son. For many people caught in immature stages of human development because of inadequate nurturing or trauma, there is no better or safer way to heal and grow up at any age than through Mary's wise loving-kindness and maternal care. She was called to the role of motherhood not only to bring up her biological son, but to continue in the role of mothering forever. She cannot cease being the mother of God or the mother of humankind. In unending visions all over the globe, described by Christians and non-Christians alike, she seems like a mother aware that infantile humankind must be brought up all over again.

Ordinarily, the mother draws out the spirit of a small child. Her warmth and embrace, her joyful facial expressions and smiles, all tell the infant how deeply he or she is loved. Just as good nourishment helps the body grow strong, so love makes the spirit grow strong. If that fails to take place or in later life needs refreshment, Mary can do what needs to be done. As St. Bernard of Clairvaux wrote some eight hundred years ago:

> Mary is like a great aqueduct that allows life-giving water to flow continually from the source to the soul.[68]

Through the mystery of her grace, the driest heart, like the most desiccated earth, can always recover its moisture and fecundity.

A crucial teaching from Step 12 for us to ponder and re-ponder is that John symbolizes us, the beloved disciples of today, and that Mary is our mother. From birth through death, there is no one who does not need a mother: a tender, supportive, comforting, strong, completely present, wise and loving mother. *We have just such a mother.* No merely human woman can be all that, but Mary is. We are indeed blessed.

REFLECTION QUESTIONS

- It was customary in the first century for a son to provide for his mother after the death of the father. Does the story shed light on Jesus' human caring and tenderness? Is that the essential message of the story, or do you think something much deeper is transpiring here?

- How did you feel reading Thich Nhat Hahn's story about "looking into your hand"? Did you look into your own hand? Did you pause to meditate on your connectedness to your own ancestors? If you continue that practice in the future, what attitude shifts might occur?

- Can you forgive the Roman soldiers for their cruelty to Jesus? Is there someone you know whom you need to forgive? Does it help to remind yourself that Mary is the universal mother of us all, including the person who hurt you? Mary has the same maternal love for that person as for each of us. It may be that Mary taught Jesus the radical value he placed on forgiving seventy times seven. Have you asked her to help you forgive?

- Does it change your view of the future to know that you have a mother you can always turn to?

ILLUMINATIONS

MARY SPEAKS TO THE BELOVED DISCIPLE:
John, disciple whom he loved,
your brother must be dead
for I feel the sword through me
as prophesied.[69]
—*Jacopone da Todi*

We need, in love, to practice only this:
letting each other go. For holding on
comes easily; we do not need to learn it.[70]
—*Rainer Maria Rilke*

Only love can generate a healing fire.
—*Source unknown*

Let nothing discourage you, nothing depress you.
Let nothing disturb your heart or your peace.
Do not be afraid of any illness, anxiety, or pain.
Am I not your mother?
Are you not safe under the protection of my mantle?
Am I not your fountain of life?
What more do you need?
—*Our Lady of Guadalupe, to Mexican visionary Juan Diego
(December 12, 1531) (adapted)*

Mary is our mother twice. She gave birth to humanity twice—
once at the Nativity, and then again at the foot of the cross.[71]
—*St. John Vianney, the Curé d'Ars, patron saint of parish priests
(1786–1859)*

PRAYERS

As it was,
As it is,
As it shall be,
Evermore. . . .
With the ebb,
With the flow.[72]
—*From* Carmina Gadelica, *Celtic prayers, Scottish Highlands,
collected by Alexander Carmichael*

My beloved Mother, if you see something in me that does not belong, help me to remove it and to make you the guide of my life and all my power. I ask you to transform everything I find displeasing in myself, and to dissipate all darkness in my soul with the light of your faith. Take my self-centeredness and replace it with love. Take my arrogance and replace it with your profound humility.

Help me to learn to ponder things in my heart as you did when you lived on this earth; may I focus and concentrate without becoming anxious or distracted. May your continual vision of God inspire me to seek his presence every day. Transform my lethargy in the light of your heart's fire, and allow your virtues to come into being in my soul. Most holy and beloved Mother, may I have a spirit like yours, to know Jesus Christ and to praise and glorify God with love like yours, forever.[73]

—*St. Louis-Marie Grignion de Montfort*

O Mary, perfect disciple of Jesus, I come to dedicate my life and my priestly ministry to you. I desire to abandon myself to the will of Jesus, your son, and walk in faith with you, my Mother. To you I consecrate my life in the priesthood. I give you every gift I possess of nature and of grace, my body and my soul, all that I own and everything I do. Pray for me that the Holy Spirit may visit me with his many gifts. Pray for me, that by faith I may know the power of Christ and by love make him present in the world. Amen.

—*Source unknown*

FREEING THE CREATIVE SPIRIT

Copy on a small Post-it note a quote that you love, such as a line of sacred poetry, a brief biblical passage, a quote from a saint, or an inspiring thought, and post it in a place where you will see it most days. You might choose the inside of a closet door where it will help you to start the day with inspiration, or the inside of a kitchen cabinet close to the coffee or tea to help quench your thirst with something spiritual.

Think of this practice as "sacred Post-its," and select beautiful messages, such as the radiant words of St. Francis of Assisi: "Praise be to you, my Lord, for Brother Sun, who is beautiful and glorious and gives us the light of day." Or this beloved verse from the Psalms: "As a deer longs for flowing streams, so my soul longs for you, O God" (42:1). Let your first posting be the beginning of a lifetime practice by continuing to post illumining quotes until you run out of surfaces. Then pack them in a box and begin all over again. Each time you run out of space, harvest your sacred Post-its and store them in the box, and you will have a treasure chest to pore over when you grow old.

The computer is not recommended for this exercise, since the instant availability of an uplifting message can be spiritually valuable on a difficult day. The computer will distance you in both time and space from the words that illumine your heart and liberate your spirit.

You might like to create a special surface in your home for sacred Post-its concerning only Mary. *The Way of Mary* offers dozens of quotes with which to begin.[74]

WAITING FOR THE SPIRIT

Mary Prays with the Disciples
in the Upper Room
for the Spirit to Come
(Acts 1:12–14)

LISTENING TO SCRIPTURE

From the Mount of Olives, as it is called, [the apostles] went back to Jerusalem, a short distance away, no more than a sabbath walk; and when they reached the city they went to the upper room where they were staying; there were Peter and John, James and Andrew, Philip and Thomas, Bartholomew and Matthew, James son of Alphaeus and Simon the Zealot, and Jude son of James. All these joined in continuous prayer, together with several women, including Mary, the mother of Jesus, and with his brothers. (Acts 1:12–14)

IMAGINING THE STORY

Summer of the year we call 33 is quickly approaching, and it is a delightfully hot day in Jerusalem. Place yourself in the upper room in the circle of disciples seated around Mary. It has been only nine days since Jesus ascended into heaven, since the disciples lost the physical sight of the light in his eyes, the sound of his voice, the joy of conversing with him at meals. And yet the spiritual beauty in this blessed room is so palpable you can almost hold it in your hand. Look at the holiness on the faces and the grace in the postures, and listen silently. Does it seem curious to you that the disciples don't appear frightened or worried, that you don't see any signs of confusion or grief? Notice that they are praying. In fact, they are deep in prayer, very close to God. It seems that Mary, who has never appeared more beautiful or serene, is leading them in prayer. The words are so clear, it is as though they were speaking in a single voice. They are praying for the Spirit of the Lord to come to them, as Jesus promised. They seem to share a single feeling: How would you describe that feeling? What are you feeling?

Before joining the community in prayer, look around at the familiar details of this cherished haven where Jesus and the inner circle so often met to debrief and plan, to rest and eat. Notice all the details you can, so you will never forget this hallowed space. What colors, textures, and aromas are there? Are the walls whitewashed? What is the furniture like where Jesus presided over his Last Supper with the apostles? Are there Roman-style couches for eating or mats, such as desert-dwellers used, or a table and benches, such as Leonardo da Vinci imagines in his painting of the Last Supper? If you picture a wooden table, is it rough and scarred or polished and handsome?

Do you think the owner of the house is well-to-do? In addition to Mary, whom do you recognize? Mary

Magdalene? Peter? The married couple Mary and Clopas? Notice how many women are there, heads veiled and graceful, with great inner strength visible on their faces. Now imagine an open window where you can look out over the surroundings; go over to it, and allow your senses to come even more alive. Are you near the center of the city or on the outskirts? What city sounds do you hear? What people, animals, birds, buildings, roads, carts, do you see? What growing things? What lies on the horizon? Now imagine that one of the men or women in the room joins you at the window and enters into a quiet conversation with you. Who is it? What does he or she say? How do you reply? Continue the conversation as long as you wish.

When you are ready, picture yourself returning to the circle, joining the others in prayer for the Spirit of Christ to come.

MEDITATIONS

On the penultimate step of *The Way of Mary*, she and a number of the other disciples are gathered in the upper room to wait for the coming of the Spirit. To wait like this is something no one has ever done before, in all the thousands of years of human history before Jesus' birth. Many spirits had been worshiped. Many cultures had believed their spirits were divine. All kinds of shamans and high priests and healers had invoked a holy spirit. But in contrast to them all, in contrast to nature worship, mystery cults, pagan religions, and ancient faiths based in

Mesopotamian goddesses, this new community waits for the Spirit of the Lord Jesus Christ. Humanity is about to meet for the first time the one true Holy Spirit of the Savior, Christ, the Son of the Living God.

Fifty days have gone by since the Resurrection, and for more than forty of those days Mary and the other disciples lived a life of unimaginable happiness reunited with the risen Lord. Every day was a holiday and a holy day of living to the fullest with Jesus, because they knew he would soon return to his Father and they would never be with him again in this way. They felt deep joy listening to new teachings—some of the most moving and beautiful of Jesus' teachings. Who could forget, for example, the morning, after he returned from the world of the dead, that he cooked breakfast for them over a fire in the open air, while the sun rose over the Sea of Galilee in a burst of luminescent reds and violets? Then he gave one his most important instructions. Like the mother of a great brood of hungry children, Jesus prepared a nourishing meal and called his disciples to come together and eat, much as he calls to us today. As he sat down on a patched white cotton blanket woven by his mother, with the familiar teaching tone of firmness and authority in his voice, he gave one last instruction in the sacred art of self-giving love. "Do you love me?" Do you really love me? Are you certain? Then, "Feed my flock" (John 21:15–17). They surely remembered his earlier teachings to clothe the homeless, welcome the immigrant, visit the sick. As you do it for one of the least of these my brothers and sisters, he had said, you do it for me. (See Matthew 25:35-40.)

Neither his mother nor the disciples will ever forget those forty days of being with the resurrected Lord. Now he is gone. Yet, strangely, despite his physical absence, they are learning one of the Lord's greatest lessons. They, and we, are learning how to wait for the Spirit of Christ. Mary is now a tried and tested woman in her forties, mature in understanding of herself and the ways of God, refined in the fires of suffering and love. She can smile tenderly while she waits for whatever will be to be. On this penultimate day of our pilgrimage with her, she exemplifies one of her most important attributes, the ability to wait with faith in the present moment, in the future, and in the world to come. For her, *all* waiting means "waiting for the Spirit." There is no empty time, no boredom, no mindless distraction or amusement, only peaceful confidence that whatever the circumstances, Christian trusting cannot end in disappointment.

Mary stands as a timeless model for all of us, men and women alike, of what it means to be spiritually complete, spiritually whole and fulfilled. If we cannot attain her absolute holiness, we can at least follow her example and grow day by day more like her. We can accept without fully understanding the strange intersection of divine plans with our own. We can smile at the mysterious way men and women's intentions can be cancelled out like items crossed off someone's list. We can wait in beauty. We can express our heart's hope. This is what Mary did. Let us do the same.

Waiting for the Spirit can be one of the holiest and most beautiful times of life. Prayer impregnates waiting with opportunity. So let us be like her, receptive and willing to wait as long as it takes, because we trust in the Word of the Lord and know in our hearts that the Spirit sent by the Christ is with us always, whether we are aware of the Holy Presence or not. Try the early community's beautiful prayer, *maranatha*: "Come, Lord Jesus, come." Then wait for the Lord, in one of his many disguises, to come.

REFLECTION QUESTIONS

- How does your attitude change when you look at waiting as "waiting for the Spirit"?
- Have you tried repetitive prayer, such as a mantra or the Rosary, while waiting?
- In what ways is praying the Rosary like being with Mary in the upper room waiting for the Spirit? Do you ever pray the Rosary while walking? If so, have you felt boredom turn into meditation?
- It has been said that a sign of maturity is the ability to postpone gratification. Do you agree? Give an example of a time when you chose to wait rather than immediately satisfy a desire. How did you feel about yourself after that choice? When do you wish you had prayed and waited more graciously? What will be your next opportunity to practice waiting like Mary?
- Have you seen a child waiting with fingers fidgeting, eyes darting around a room, impatience rising toward the bursting point? That is an appropriate behavior for a child, but some adults behave in the same way. Do you know such a person? Do you ever feel that way?

ILLUMINATIONS

I am watching all the roads,
I am thirsting for your love,
O my beloved.
—*Mahadevi, India, twelfth century*

Ages pass, and still Thou pourest,
and still there is room to fill.[75]
—*Rabindranath Tagore, India (1861–1941)*

My soul yearns for you in the night;
yes, my spirit within me keeps vigil for you.
—*Isaiah 26:9*

Let nothing disturb you.
Let nothing dismay you.
All things pass.
God never changes.
Patience attains
all that it strives for.
Those who have God
find they lack nothing.
God alone suffices.[76]
—*St. Teresa of Avila, Carmelite sister and reformer
(1515–1582)*

PRAYERS

Enter and penetrate,
O Spirit. Come and bless
This hour.[77]
—*Madeleine L'Engle, contemporary Anglican writer*

Lord, send your dew upon this sterile earth
and it will return to life.[78]
—*A prayer about Mary by Blessed Miriam Baouardy,*
Lebanese nun (1846–1878)

PRAYER TO OUR LADY OF FIFTH AVENUE

I come to you, Holy Mother,
to ask your prayers for _____.

You give us all encouragement to approach you
as your children, whose brother, your son,
Jesus Christ, we claim as our blessed Savior
and yours.

Help me now, I ask you, with a prayer
to Him on my behalf and for His sake.
Amen.
—*Prayer accompanying a statue of Mary and Jesus*
dedicated at St. Thomas (Episcopal) Church,
Fifth Avenue, New York City, 1991

Sancta Maria, Ora pro Nobis![79]
Pray, O Mother, for all of us.
Pray for humanity that suffers poverty and injustice,
violence and hatred, terror and war.
Help us to contemplate with the holy rosary
the mysteries of God who is our peace.
So that we will feel involved
in a specific effort of service to peace.

Look with special attention
upon the land in which you gave birth to Jesus,
a land that you loved together
and that is still so tried today.
Pray for us, Mother of Hope.
Give us days of peace, watch over our way.
Let us see your son
full of joy in heaven! Amen.
—*Pope John Paul II, in a sermon delivered
on the Feast of the Immaculate Conception,
December 8, 2002*

FREEING THE CREATIVE SPIRIT

Create an image of Mary in her forties, at the height of her maturity and feminine power, strong in every way and full of wisdom. Remember that the forties in her era were equivalent to the sixties today, and she had reached true maturity. These were years of reaping the harvest that Jesus had sowed in her heart for well over thirty years, from the moment his life on earth took form inside herself and she began her lifelong search for understanding of just who her son was. She journeyed with her child as he grew to manhood, and walked with him while he taught the world about love and what God is really like. She was at his side when he died, and found him again in his resurrected body. And when he ascended into heaven, she had to recover for the second time from the terrible loss of his physical presence. Now the mother of Jesus walked a path that centuries later would be named "the way of the Cross" and "the way of the Resurrection," cherishing her son's spiritual presence in her heart. In the burgeoning Christian community, she was honored and loved as a source of his light.

But there is much more to Mary in her forties than memories and her friends' affection. Think about the impact of all the people she met and all the profound or joyous or painful events she underwent. Think about choices she made. Think about the outcome of her prayer life after so many years. How did it all affect who she was at this time of fruition and fulfillment? Ask yourself questions like these before you begin fashioning your image of Mary in maturity.

When you are ready, use any medium you like: a computer, paper and pencil or colored pens; watercolors or oils. Make a Mary collage; sew a Mary doll; sculpt in clay; carve in wood. Use symbols if you like. A woman who embroidered a large, full-color image of Our Lady of Guadalupe on a red dress opens another world of possibilities for you if you like to sew. You could embroider your picture of Mary on a piece of clothing, knit it into a scarf or sweater, or represent it on a quilt. If you prefer, copy one of the famous images of Mary in art that matches, more or less, your own picture of her. Or depict her in one of her hundreds of titles, such as Queen of Heaven or Mother of the Church. Many of her titles begin with Our Lady of _____, bringing Mary into relationship with nature—such as Our Lady of the Sea, Our Lady of the Snows, Our Lady of the Woods, and many others.

A woman sewed the words "Hail Mary, full of grace, the Lord is with you" like a necklace on a white dress. This approach suggests a number of additional possibilities for freeing the creative spirit. Words that Mary spoke, or that someone has said or written about her, or your own words about her, could be sewed or painted or carved to symbolize her mature presence.

Please keep in mind that it is absolutely unnecessary to have a special gift or talent in any means of expression to enjoy this practice.

STEP 14
PENTECOST

*The Spirit of Mary's Son Brings Sacred Gifts
of Wisdom and Speech*
(Acts 2:1–4)

LISTENING TO SCRIPTURE

*When Pentecost day came around, they had all met in one
room, when suddenly they heard what sounded like a powerful
wind from heaven, the noise of which filled the entire house where
they were sitting; and something appeared to them that seemed
like tongues of fire; these separated and rested on the heads of
each of them. They were all filled with the Holy Spirit and
began to speak in other tongues as the Spirit gave them the gift
of speech. (Acts 2:1–4)*

IMAGINING THE STORY

The last step of our pilgrimage with Mary finds her
on another hot day at the end of spring in the year we
call 33, again seated in the upper room. Mary is deep
in prayer, and her striking posture is a living portrait of
feminine wisdom in a spirit set totally free. Her back is as
straight as a cedar, her head gracefully bowed, her dark eyes
fixed on a distant vision of something no one else can see.

Seated on mats close to her are women and men from the earliest circle of Jesus' disciples, whom she dearly loves.

The eleven apostles remaining since Judas' suicide are seated around a long table. Unusually excited, oscillating between joy and fear in anticipation of the monumental event that is coming momentarily, they are praying fervently. Imagine that you are there in the upper room, praying with Mary that the Spirit will come quickly. What will this be like for the apostles? What more can happen after all the wonders and miracles of Jesus' ministry? Everyone in the room, including you, witnessed all kinds of "signs," one amazing healing after another, even Jesus' return from death! How can anything add to what has already happened?

But as the hours fly by, those present find themselves praying more and more fervently, as though some invisible, pressing energy is building and reaching toward a crescendo. In your imagination, can you picture yourself there in the upper room praying with such anticipation? Notice all the details of your surroundings so you can remember this day forever. Are you sitting on a reed mat? Did you remove your sandals before entering this sacred space? What is your prayer?

Can you picture yourself looking at Mary and seeing a flame of fire burning just above her head? Look at James and see a flame above his head, too. Then Andrew and Bartholomew: flames are hovering over them, too, and over everyone else. Something wondrous and glorious, much more powerful than anyone anticipated, is happening.

Now all at once their voices burst out in mysterious, jubilant sounds in languages no one knows, like a choir of angels singing in perfect harmony to praise God. If you were there, what would you be feeling? Do you think you understand what a precious gift has been given? Imagine yourself, when things settle down in the upper room, conversing with Mary about the descent of the Spirit. What do you say to her? How does she respond? Continue the conversation.

MEDITATIONS

On the last stage of our pilgrimage with Mary, an energy of tremendous beauty and holiness fills the upper room. Mary's face is suffused with love, and the apostles appear transported. They have been praying for a long time, with such strong longing and belief that love is flooding their hearts, and they are as close as human beings can come to the veil that separates heaven and earth. They are on the immediate brink of the great divine breakthrough of Pentecost. Although future Christians, such as we, will know many powerful Pentecost-like events, nothing will ever again approach the descent of the Spirit of Jesus Christ in the upper room. Even the mother of Jesus, who graces this sacred space with her special blessedness, and the dozen chosen men who will faithfully follow her son all the way to the end of their lives, have no idea that gifts received on this day are beginning the outreach of the church to the ends of the known world. The apostles will be able to take Jesus to the people of every land.

One of the many implicit teachings in step 14 is about prayer and spiritual experience inspiring outreach to others. We ourselves know from our own blessed times of spiritual experience that the life of prayer leads to love. Love can well up when we least expect it, and can grow, build, and crescendo in timeless seconds or minutes into longing to serve and give and change the world, as did the apostles at Pentecost and the saints throughout the centuries.

This sequence from prayer to love to service is the experience of St. Catherine of Siena (1340–1444), who spent three years in solitary prayer before turning to nursing the poor, preaching publicly, and counseling the pope. St. Catherine of Genoa (1447–1510) was energized by intense spiritual experience to undertake selfless hospital work. St. Teresa of Avila (1515–1582) was led to found sixteen convents, and St. John of the Cross (1542–1591) was inspired to write breathtaking poetry. The intellectual giant St. Thomas Aquinas (1226–1274) had a profound Pentecost-like experience at the end of his life that took him in another direction: He stopped writing and told his students to burn his *Summa*.[80] In comparison to knowing Christ, he concluded, "My work is but straw."

Closer to our own time, this moving description of a spiritual experience was written by Rabbi Abraham Joshua Heschel:

> In every life there are moments when there is a lifting of the veil at the horizon of the known, opening a sight of the eternal. Each of us has at least once in life experienced the momentous reality of God. Each of us has once caught a glimpse of the beauty, peace, and power that flow through the souls of those who are devoted to God. But such experiences are rare events. To some people they are like shooting stars, passing and unremembered. In others they kindle a light that is never quenched.[81]

Epiphanies, whether quiet or blindingly beautiful, are not reserved for mystics.

Let us return to the year 33, when at last the long-awaited Spirit of Christ descends in a rush of symbolic riches, an indefinable sound like roaring winds and a downpour of mystical flames that drench the apostles, body and soul, with wisdom and new knowledge and amazing gifts. It is as though an explosion in heaven has forced open the skies to release the last torrential powers that the community needs to take Jesus to the ends of the earth. When the great Spirit-storm subsides, those called to this fiery baptism in the Spirit suddenly burst out speaking in tongues like excited children just learning to talk. Their minds and hearts are aflame; their spirits burn with faith and love and dedication to following the path of Christ—wherever it takes them and whatever the cost.

With Pentecost, Mary disappears out of sight in the New Testament. But she enters a sacred place in the heart and memory of the young community that grows brighter and brighter with the passing years. Ever more loved and revered, more written about and prayed to, she eventually, in the fifth century, enters human awareness as the beloved Mother of God. Ever after, even during the darkest days of church history, Mary remains a wholly reliable source of solace and peace, a blessed mother for everyone.

REFLECTION QUESTIONS

- For many scholars today, it is unthinkable that Mary would not be present to receive the Spirit sent by her own son—especially since the New Testament places Mary in the upper room in the days between the Ascension and Pentecost, waiting and praying with a number of Jesus' followers for the coming of the Spirit (Acts 1:14). The text, however, does not mention her by name as having been present. What do you think about this?

- The essential "gift of the Spirit" on Pentecost was a complex gift of speech, understanding, and special wisdom. The Bible mentions dozens more. The prophet Isaiah lists six "gifts of the Spirit": wisdom, insight, counsel, strength, knowledge, and awe before God (11:2), to which the New Testament adds a seventh: devotion. St. Paul mentions faith, hope, love, compassion, leadership, and many others. Think of a gift of the Spirit that characterizes you. Think of a gift of the Spirit that you wish characterized you.

- To what extent can these "gifts of the Spirit" be seen as "gifts," and to what extent must we prepare or exert ourselves to receive them?

- Some people understand the "gift of speech" received by the disciples on Pentecost as the ability to speak foreign languages, while others believe the disciples spoke in unknown tongues. What is your opinion? Have you ever been in a Christian charismatic community when members spoke in tongues? If so, what was the experience like for you?

- Have you ever had what you would call a spiritual experience? One test of the genuineness of a spiritual experience resides in the outcome: good comes out of an authentic experience. Did good come out of yours? Who benefited?

ILLUMINATIONS

I found the world wrapped in an inexpressible glory with its waves of joy and beauty bursting and breaking on all sides. The thick cloud of sorrow that lay on my heart in many folds was pierced through and through by the light of the world, which was everywhere radiant. . . . There was nothing and no one whom I did not love at that moment.[82]

—Rabindranath Tagore, India (1861–1941)

Forever at his door
I gave my heart and soul. My fortune, too.
I've no flock anymore,
no other work in view.
My occupation: love. It's all I do.[83]
—St. John of the Cross, sixteenth-century mystic

I was seized with a feeling of familiarity with God, with Jesus, with Mary. . . . I wept and exulted. It was as if there were a perpetual spring of joy, of sweetness, of happy certainty welling up in me—it lasted a long while—and the memory of it has never been effaced.[84]
—Raissa Maritain, Russian contemplative (1883–1960)

How could you go on sleeping
when all of us are awake?
Speak now, and join us.
Hear our song.[85]

—*Andal, Indian mystic, eighth century*

[Y]ou will receive the power of the Holy Spirit
which will come on you,
and then you will be my witnesses
not only in Jerusalem but throughout Judea and Samaria,
and indeed to earth's remotest end.

—*Acts 1:8*

PRAYERS

Mary, my dearest mother,
give me your heart
so beautiful, so pure, so immaculate,
so full of love and humility.
That I may receive Jesus as you did,
and go in haste to give him to others.
—*Blessed Mother Teresa of Calcutta*

O Mary, in your heart, I have found life.[86]
—*Blessed Mariam Baouardy, Lebanese nun (1846–1878)*

What shall I say to you, my God? Shall I collect together
all the words that praise your holy name, shall I give you all
the names of this world, You, the Unnamable? Shall I call You
God of my life, meaning of my existence, hallowing of my
acts, my journey's end, bitterness of my bitter hours, home
of my loneliness, You my most treasured happiness? Shall I
say Creator, Sustainer, Pardoner, Near One, Distant One,
Incomprehensible One, God both of flowers and stars, God of
the gentle wind and of terrible battles, Wisdom, Power, Loyalty,
and Truthfulness, Eternity and Infinity, You, the All-Merciful,
You the Just One, You Love itself?[87]

—*Karl Rahner, twentieth-century priest and theologian, Germany*

FREEING THE CREATIVE SPIRIT

The fourteen steps or stages of *The Way of Mary* highlight many of Mary's personal strengths, virtues, values, and character traits that have made her the perfect spiritual model for men and women since the earliest years of the Christian community. She is everything the human heart aspires to be, and she lives the way we all truly want to live, without remorse, free of guilt, never harming the soul of another woman or man. Mary never has to retract a word she has spoken nor ask to be forgiven. In every relationship and role God calls her to—as a woman, wife, and mother; as her future teacher's teacher; as a deep thinker; as a prophet; or as a saint—she serves God's purposes wholeheartedly, bravely, lovingly. She alone of all people who will ever live spends some thirty-three years in direct, uninterrupted company with the Lord Jesus Christ, the Son of God. She is the Mother of God. Who better than Mary could be the spiritual model for humankind? Who better than she can bring out the image and likeness of her son in each of us?

Now, as you complete the final practice in the final step of your pilgrimage with Mary, look back on the virtues and strengths you have seen her exemplify throughout *The Way of Mary*. In Step 1, the Annunciation, there is her ability to let go of fear. In Steps 2 and 3, when Mary and Elizabeth greet one another, there is the radiance of her joy. At the wedding party of Cana in Step 10, her assertiveness is striking.

Prepare a list of at least a dozen of these soul qualities. What comes to mind first of all? And second? Third? Now, keep going.

It is likely you have significantly updated your image of Mary through the scriptural passages and practices in this book and that you see her differently today. Be sure to include on your list some of the characteristics that surprised you. Include, also, those you would most like to see in yourself. It is crucial to remember that whatever these may be, Mary can help bring them out in you. *The path that she has left us is a path that we can follow.*

Be sure to keep your list to compare it with the new list you prepare the next time you complete *The Way of Mary*. You may be surprised at how far you have come on her path of transforming faith and love.

AFTER YOU READ THIS BOOK

IT MAY HAVE OCCURRED TO YOU while practicing the steps in this book that *The Way of Mary* resembles *The Way of the Cross* and *The Way of the Resurrection*. All three devotions consist of fourteen stations—although *The Way of Mary* calls them steps—that originate in the New Testament. The great difference is that the first two devotions focus on Jesus, while the one proposed in this book dwells on his mother.

The stations of the cross, or *Via Crucis* (pronounced "veea crutchis"), which appear on the walls of every Catholic Church, commemorate fourteen events from the day of Jesus' crucifixion. Throughout the year, but especially during Lent, Catholics walk the way of the cross in a church or garden, stopping at each station to ponder Christ's suffering and to pray. The practice may have originated in the first century. One ancient tradition holds that after Jesus' death, Mary would walk the path from the Garden of Olives where Jesus was apprehended, to the court of the high priest where he was tried, then on to the Praetorium for the confrontation with Pontius Pilate, and eventually to the hill of Golgotha. (See John 18:1–19:18.) We know that a few hundred years later, pilgrims were coming to Jerusalem from far away to walk the sacred path, sometimes on their knees in repentance for sins. The Way of the Cross ranged from only three stations during some eras to over forty at other times; only in 1731 did Pope Clement XII fix the number at fourteen.

It remains a mystery why a spiritual practice beginning and ending in Jesus' agony without any reference to the Resurrection was perpetuated for so long. But happily in the 1990s, a spiritual group in Italy, guided by a Salesian priest and scholar, Rev. Sabino Palumbieri, combined fourteen joyous events from the post–Resurrection season into a beautiful new devotion, the Way of the Resurrection, or *Via Lucis* (pronounced "veea lootchis"). These fourteen events are called "The Stations of the Light."[88]

It was my intention to suggest with this book that adding a *Via Mariae* to the *Via Crucis* and *Via Lucis* could bring a partial path to completion.

Together, the three "Ways" bring to life the full masculine and feminine beauty, majesty, and mystery of the Christian story, which the *Via Crucis* and *Via Lucis* alone cannot do. Completing the sorrowful Way of the Cross and the joyful Way of the Resurrection with the missing dimension of the sacred feminine is like restoring the original colors, sheen, and life to an ancient icon, or retouching a black and white film with color.

Today, the Way of Light is finding its way into churches and parish gardens in the form of uplifting pictures and sculptures; they bring into balance the suffering, evil, sin, and guilt depicted on the Way of the Cross with the faith, love, joy, and goodness of the post-Easter life of the risen

Lord. If a formal Way of Mary were to be created and brought into relationship with the other two "Ways," it would surely nurture reverence for Mary and bring about increased devotion to Jesus Christ, her son, to whom she always points us, and of whom she always says, "Do as he tells you."

# ACKNOWLEDGMENTS

A THOUSAND THANKS TO ALL THE WONDERFUL PEOPLE AT PARACLETE PRESS and in the Community of Jesus, especially Jon Sweeney, a consummate editor and a beacon of light in the world; Robert Edmonson, for the monumental amount of time and insight contributed to this book; Anna Mitchell for the loveliness of her illustrations and design; every member of the publishing team, for the joy of being with you on June 20, 2007, and the spiritual beauty you brought to our work together; Pamela Jordan for special kindness; Sr. Estelle, Sr. Helen, and Christy for loving hospitality that is truly Benedictine; and Lil Copan, whose poetic soul has been a blessing on our long journey with Mary.

It is impossible to complete this book without mentioning the faculty, administration, and staff at Princeton Theological Seminary, especially the teachers who taught me to "think theologically"—with faith and love: Dr. David Willis, Dr. Karlfried Froelich, and Drs. Donald Juel and James Loder (in memoriam). Thank you for exemplifying and nurturing in me "the love of learning and the desire for God."

My thanks go also to the library staffs at Harvard Divinity School, Andover Newton Theological School, and Boston College for kind assistance with research.

I owe the deepest gratitude possible to my family, who have remained close to me through all the pages of this book: to Axel Grabowsky, my lifetime beloved, for the outstanding research skills, striving mind, and love of learning that you have shared with me throughout this project; to Tara Grabowsky, for your love, insights, and incomparable support, and for the beauty of the sacred feminine that you embody and brought to discussions about this book; and to Kevin Potts, for thoughtful advice about this book, and for the integrity, faith, and intellect that I heard in that advice.

Thanks also to dear friends: Sr. Jose Hobday, CSF, the only saint I have ever known, a holy woman who has poured phenomenal power into writing, lecturing, serving the poor, and capturing the hearts of thousands of people, including my own. Thank you, beloved Sister, for all our "holy hours" discussing Mary and for gracing our planet and my life with your wise words. Thanks as well to Paola Biola, for the strength and love in your weekly if not daily encouragement; for sharing with me your vast understanding of Mary, your love for her and for Marian art, and your great library; and for being the most a friend can be, a guardian of the soul.

# CREDITS

Biblical citations were taken from *The New Oxford Annotated Bible, Revised Standard Version*, eds. Herbert G. May and Bruce M. Metzger, published and copyright © 1973 by Oxford University Press, Inc. New York City; *The Jerusalem Bible,* copyright © 1968 by Darton, Longman & Todd Ltd and Doubleday and Company, Inc., published by Doubleday and Company, Inc. Garden City, New York; and *The New Jerusalem Bible,* copyright © 1985 by Darton, Longman & Todd Ltd. and Doubleday, published by Doubleday, New York City. My preference for one translation over another depended generally on its fidelity to the original Greek or Hebrew. In some cases, the selection was based on the beauty of the language.

Psalms were taken from *The Christian Community Bible* © 1995 by Bernardo Hurault, published by Claretian Publications, Quezon City, Philippines, and by Liguori Publications, Liguori, Missouri.

I am grateful to Paraclete Press for permission to use "Prayer to Our Lady of Fifth Avenue," which appeared in Jon Sweeney's *The Lure of Saints: A Protestant Experience of Catholic Tradition* (2005); to M. P. A. Schaeffer for kind permission to reprint *Ti Prego*; and to Dorothy Walters for permission to reprint her poem "What Is Happening?" from *Marrow of Flame: Poems of the Spiritual Journey* (Prescott, AZ: Hohm Press, 2000).

NOTES

1. In even the poorest cities of Mexico, for example, on December 12, the Feast of Our Lady of Guadalupe, people stand in line for hours to attend jubilant all-night masses where they can sing and praise and celebrate their beloved patron saint with unrestrained fervor and faith, for a few hours forgetful of their suffering.

2. Inevitably, problems arise from using this method, as in Step 9, when Mary and Joseph become refugees to save the infant Jesus from Herod's killings. This would appear to take place in the year 2, yet it is known that Herod the Great died in 4 BC. Therefore, dating tends to be misleading, but ultimately in this book, that is irrelevant; what matters is following Mary on her path of transforming love.

3. This remark appeared in the Dec. 23, 2005 edition of *The Economist*.

4. See *In Search of Mary: The Woman and the Symbol* (New York: Ballantine Books, 1996).

5. Her silence when shepherds suddenly appeared after Jesus' birth offers a good example of this.

6. Cardinal Nicolas of Cusa (1401–1464), who won fame for his learning and love of God, was a Christian Platonist

inspired by one of the greatest Christian mystics of all time, Blessed John Ruysbroeck (1293–1381). Both came from Flanders. See Nicolas of Cusa, *The Vision of God*, trans. by E. Gurney Salter (London/New York: J. M. Dent & Sons, Ltd./E. P. Dutton & Co., 1928).

7. See my book *WomanPrayers* (San Francisco: HarperSanFrancisco, 2003).

8. Taken from Dorothy Walters, *Marrow of Flame: Poems of the Spiritual Journey* (Prescott, AZ: Hohm Press, 2000). Used with the author's permission.

9. This thought is developed in *Mary: The Imagination of Her Heart* by Penelope Duckworth (Cambridge, MA: Cowley, 2004).

10. Translated by Coleman Barks.

11. From the *Duino Elegies*. See *The Selected Poetry of Rainer Maria Rilke,* ed. and trans. by Stephen Mitchell (New York: Random House, 1980).

12. See Mary Oliver, *Dream Work* (New York: Atlantic Monthly Press, 1986).

13. From *Anam Cara: A Book of Celtic Wisdom* by John O'Donohue (New York: HarperCollins, 1997).

14. Sri Eknath Easwaran founded The Blue Mountain Center of Meditation in Petaluma, CA. The Center has been guided since his death by his wife and continues to offer meditation retreats in the U.S. and Europe. This remark appeared in a recent edition of the Center's newsletter.

15. Quoted in *Women in Praise of the Sacred*, ed. Jane Hirshfield (New York: HarperCollins, 1994.)

16. Translator unknown. Bishop Gregory of Neocaesarea in Asia Minor was named "Thaumaturgos," or "Wonder-worker," because of his widespread conversion of pagans to Christianity. He is venerated as a saint in the Russian and Greek Orthodox churches. His writings can be found in J.-P. Migne, ed., *Patrologiae cursus completus: series graeca*, 162 vols. (Paris, 1857–66).

17. See Dag Hammarskjöld's spiritual classic, *Markings* (New York City: Alfred A. Knopf, 1964).

18. Translator unknown.

19. Translator unknown.

20. Author's translation. See Hildegard von Bingen, *Lieder [Symphonia armonie celestium revelationem]*, ed. by Prudentiana Barth, M.-I. Ritscher, and Joseph Schmidt-Goerg (Salzburg: Otto Mueller Verlag, 1969). The eagle here probably symbolizes the contemplative.

21. This title comes from Adriana Diaz.

22. This idea, which appears in many versions and writings, is traceable to the great writer on friendship, the Cistercian monk Aelred of Rievaulx (1110–67), but likely originates much earlier. "Saint" Aelred, like "Saint" Hildegard of Bingen, was never formally canonized. (Hildegard failed the canonization process three times.) The title is an honorific attributable to their mutual popularity.

23. See Simone Weil, *Waiting for God,* trans. by Emma Craufurd (New York: G. P. Putnam's Sons, 1951); also *Selected Essays 1934-1943,* chosen and translated by Richard Rees (London: Oxford University Press, 1962).

24. Translator unknown.

25. See Macrina Wiederkehr, *A Tree Full of Angels: Seeing the Holy in the Ordinary* (San Francisco: HarperSanFrancisco, 1988.)

26. Translator unknown.

27. Herbert O'Driscoll, *Portrait of a Woman: Meditations on the Mother of Our Lord* (Toronto, ON, Canada: The Anglican Book Centre, 1981), 37.

28. From the compact disc *Drops of Emptiness: Songs, Chants, and Poetry from Plum Village, France* (Boulder, CO: Sounds True, 1997).

29. This is a fragment from the prolific exegetical writer and hymnist St. Ephrem of Syria, a Desert Father whose preaching eloquence earned him renown as the "harp of the Holy Spirit." He spent his last decade of life in solitary contemplation.

30. Few saints have exhibited a more sublime devotion to Mary than St. Francis. See *Francis and Clare: The Complete Works,* translation and introduction by Regis J. Armstrong, OFM CAP, and Ignatius Brady, OFM, in *The Classics of Western Spirituality* (Mahwah, NJ: Paulist Press, 1982).

31. See St. Catherine of Siena, *The Dialogue,* translation and introduction by Suzanne Noffke, OP, in *The Classics of Western Spirituality* (Mahwah, NJ: Paulist Press, 1980).

32. See my book, *Spiritual Writings on Mary* (Woodstock, VT: Skylight Paths Publishing, 2005).

33. The image comes from the time of Dante and Rumi.

34. Prayed by Thich Naht Hahn at a retreat given with Sr. Chan Khong in Oakland, CA, 1996.

35. Quoted in Ronda De Sola Chervin, *Prayers of the Women Mystics* (Ann Arbor, MI: Servant Publications, 1992).

36. One version of the Golden Rule states: "Do to others as you would have others do to you."

37. See Philip Armstrong, csc, *Your Own Mysteries: Praying Your Life Through the Rosary* (Notre Dame, IN: Ave Maria Press, 2004).

38. For a more thorough discussion of these ideas, see books by scholars in the Jesus Seminar, such as Marcus J. Borg's *Meeting Jesus Again for the First Time: The Historical Jesus and the Heart of Contemporary Faith* (San Francisco: HarperSanFrancisco, 1994).

39. Penelope Duckworth's words, in *Mary: The Imagination of Her Heart* (Cambridge, MA: Cowley, 2004).

40. This idea is developed by Beverly Roberts Gaventa in *Mary: Glimpses of the Mother of Jesus* (Minneapolis, MN: Fortress, 1999). See also *Blessed One: Protestant Perspectives on Mary,* ed. by Beverly Roberts Gaventa and Cynthia L. Rigby (Louisville, KY: Westminster John Knox, 2002).

41. According to the book of Hebrews, the practice of animal sacrifice to atone for sins became obsolete after Jesus offered himself once and for all for the forgiveness of sins (7:26–27; 9:11–10:18). Jesus offered forgiveness without the requirement of belonging to

the temple structure, implying that butcher-priests and ritual slaughter, which belonged to the era of the old covenant, were not needed in the time of the new covenant. Love has fulfilled the law (Romans 13:10). "You yourselves are God's temple," St. Paul says (1 Corinthians 3:16), to signal the real locus of love. Jesus' criticism of the temple and the priestly hierarchy in first-century Palestine suggests a rejection of *all* animal sacrifice for religious purposes (such as peace offerings or thanksgiving), not only that intended for atonement.

42. Macrina Wiederkehr, *A Tree Full of Angels*.

43. This psalm is part of the Little Office of Mary.

44. There is a discussion of flowers associated with Mary in Jon Sweeney's book, *Strange Heaven: The Virgin Mary as Woman, Mother, Disciple, and Advocate* (Brewster, MA: Paraclete Press, 2006), 139–41.

45. See Luke 2:29–30. Anna antedates a role played by another holy woman, Mary Magdalene, some thirty years later. Mary Magdalene will *proclaim the Resurrection*. Just as Anna is singled out at the beginning of Jesus' life to proclaim his birth, Mary Magdalene is chosen at the end, above all other apostles and disciples, male or female, to tell the world that he is risen from the dead (John 20:18). These parallel actions by two important women hold immense, untapped significance and symbolic value for Christian history in light of the relative paucity in the Gospels of female influence. Anna was beloved by God and held in highest esteem

by the people because of her reputation as a prophet, the most respected level in life a woman in her culture could attain. Extra-canonical writings, such as the *Gospel of Mary*, indicate that Mary Magdalene was held in high regard by Jesus, and became a wise leader in the early Jesus movement. Each of these two strong women, one old and one young, brought women's nurturing love and support to Jesus' mother. Anna stood with her at the beginning of Jesus' life; Mary Magdalene was there at the end.

46. Yeats imagines Mary struggling to understand how her son is both human and divine.

47. This verse recalls Anna's choice of lifestyle when she moved to the temple to fast and pray.

48. *Ti prego* in Italian is the equivalent of "I plead with you," or "I pray you."

49. Published in my book, *WomanPrayers*.

50. See Raissa Maritain, *Raissa's Journal*, presented by Jacques Maritain (Albany, NY: Magi Books, 1974).

51. There is considerable confusion pertaining to the various "Marys" in the New Testament. Mary and Martha are the sisters of Lazarus and lived in Bethany. See John 11:1.

52. Søren Kierkegaard, *Purity of Heart Is to Will One Thing* (New York: Harper & Row, 1938), 28.

53. Excerpted from a poem in Pope John Paul II's *Collected Poems*, trans. by Jerzy Peterkiewicz (New York: Random House, 1987).

54. See *Catherine of Genoa, Purgation and Purgatory; The Spiritual Dialogue*, translated by Serge Hughes and

introduced by Benedict J. Groeschel, in *The Classics of Western Spirituality* (Mahwah, NJ: Paulist Press, 1979).

55. Material from Blessed Mary of Agreda taken from Chervin, *Prayers of the Women Mystics.*

56. See Blaise Pascal, *Pensées*, translated by W. F. Trotter and introduced by T. S. Eliot (Mineola, NY: Dover Publications, 2003).

57. Translator unknown.

58. Translator unknown.

59. *Ave Regina* is Latin for "Hail, Queen"; *Ave Maris Stella* means "Hail, Star of the Sea."

60. From the *Uncollected Poems* of Rainer Maria Rilke, in Mitchell, ed., *The Selected Poems.*

61. This masterpiece from a lawyer who entered the second generation of Franciscans and became a spiritual genius is a fragment of Jacopone's powerful meditation on the Passion. The translator of this version is unknown.

62. From his poem "Requiem," in Mitchell, ed., *The Selected Poems.*

63. See Stephen Mitchell, *A Book of Psalms*, selected and adapted from the Hebrew (New York: Harper Collins, 1993).

64. Translator unknown.

65. Rashani, an Eastern spiritual name, gave this poem to friends before moving to a hermitage in an unknown location some years ago. She now has a spiritual center in Ka'alehu, HI, the Kipukamaluhia sanctuary, where she offers retreats. See www.rashani.com.

66. See Thomas à Kempis, *Imitation of Christ*, translated by Ronald Knox and Michael Oakley (San Francisco: Ignatius, 2005).

67. See Thich Nhat Hanh, *The Sun My Heart* (Berkeley, CA: Parallax Press, 1988).

68. To better understand Bernard of Clairvaux and the other monks and nuns mentioned in *The Way of Mary*, see *The Love of Learning and the Desire for God: A Study of Monastic Culture,* by the brilliant Benedictine Jean Leclercq, translated by Catharine Misrahi (New York: Fordham University Press, 1982).

69. See note 61.

70. From "Requiem," in Mitchell, ed., *The Selected Poems.*

71. See Andrew Harvey and Eryk Hanut, *Mary's Vineyard: Daily Meditations, Readings, and Revelations* (Wheaton, IL: Quest Books, 1996).

72. See *Carmina Gadelica (Ortha Nan Gaidheal),* vols. I–V, compiled by Alexander Carmichael, 1900–1954 (Edinburgh, Scotland: Scottish Academic Press, 1970).

73. Author's translation.

74. For a more thorough discussion of this practice, see my book *Sacred Voices: Essential Women's Wisdom Through the Ages* (San Francisco: HarperSanFrancisco, 2002), 1–4.

75. See Rabindranath Tagore, *Gitanjali: A Collection of Indian Songs* (New York: Macmillan, 1971).

76. One of St. Teresa's most famous exhortations to her Carmelite sisters, this prayer was on her bookmark.

77. See Madeleine L'Engle with Carole F. Chase, *Glimpses of Grace: Daily Thoughts and Reflections* (San Francisco: HarperSanFrancisco, 1998).

78. See Chervin, *Prayers of the Women Mystics.*

79. *Sancta Maria, Ora pro Nobis* is Latin for "Holy Mary, pray for us."

80. St. Thomas's students compiled the last book in his sixty-volume *Summa Theologica.*

81. See Rabbi Abraham Joshua Heschel, *Quest for God: Studies in Prayer and Symbolism* (New York: Crossroad, 1987).

82. Tagore, *Gitanjali.*

83. Stanza 28 of *The Spiritual Canticle,* which St. John of the Cross wrote in prison. It is an expression of his own mystical experience.

84. Maritain, *Raissa's Journal.*

85. Author's translation.

86. Chervin, *Prayers of the Women Mystics.*

87. In this beautiful prayer, Karl Rahner, SJ, presses against the limits of language to describe the God of Jesus, whom he has come to know in contemplative prayer. See my book *Prayers for All People* (New York: Doubleday, 1995). The prayer was read at a 1995 reformed worship service. Go online to www.reformedworship.org/magaazine/article.cfm?art.

88. See my book *Stations of the Light* (New York: Doubleday, 2005).

ABOUT PARACLETE PRESS

WHO WE ARE

Paraclete Press is an ecumenical publisher of books and recordings on Christian spirituality. Our publishing represents a full expression of Christian belief and practice—from Catholic to Evangelical, from Protestant to Orthodox.

Paraclete Press is the publishing arm of the Community of Jesus, an ecumenical monastic community in the Benedictine tradition. As such, we are uniquely positioned in the marketplace without connection to a large corporation and with informal relationships to many branches and denominations of faith.

We like it best when people buy our books from booksellers, our partners in successfully reaching as wide an audience as possible.

WHAT WE ARE DOING

Books

Paraclete Press publishes books that show the richness and depth of what it means to be Christian. Although Benedictine spirituality is at the heart of all that we do, we publish books that reflect the Christian experience across many cultures, time periods, and houses of worship.

We publish books that nourish the vibrant life of the church and its people— books about spiritual practice, formation, history, ideas, and customs.

We have several different series of books within Paraclete Press, including the best-selling Living Library series of modernized classic texts; A Voice from the Monastery—giving voice to men and women monastics about what it means to live a spiritual life today; award-winning literary faith fiction; and books that explore Judaism and Islam and discover how these faiths inform Christian thought and practice.

Recordings

From Gregorian chant to contemporary American choral works, our music recordings celebrate the richness of sacred choral music through the centuries. Paraclete is proud to distribute the recordings of the internationally acclaimed choir Gloriæ Dei Cantores, who have been praised for their "rapt and fathomless spiritual intensity" by *American Record Guide,* and the Gloriæ Dei Cantores Schola, which specializes in the study and performance of Gregorian chant. Paraclete is also the exclusive North American distributor of the recordings of the Monastic Choir of St. Peter's Abbey in Solesmes, France, long considered to be a leading authority on Gregorian chant performance.

Learn more about us at our Web site:
www.paracletepress.com,
or call us toll-free at 1-800-451-5006.

ALSO RECOMMENDED

The Lost Gospel of Mary:
The Mother of Jesus
in Three Ancient Texts
By Frederica Mathewes-Green

ISBN: 978-1-55725-536-5
Price: $19.95
Hardcover, 159 pages

Some have piled her status so high that it rivals that of her Son. Others do their best to ignore her entirely. Behind all of these images there is still a girl who grew up to become the mother of Christ. Frederica Mathewes-Green opens up Mary's life before the Nativity, offering a window into her centrality to Christian faith in new and sometimes startling ways.

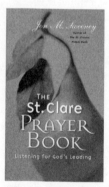

The St. Clare Prayer Book:
Listening for God's Leading
By Jon M. Sweeney

ISBN: 978-1-55725-513-6
Price: $15.95
French fold, 193 pages

Discover the spirituality of St. Clare and how it complements that of St. Francis. Enter into a week of morning and evening prayer centered on themes from Clare's life. Pray with Clare's own words in a variety of occasions. And enjoy a special appendix that dramatizes what it might have been like to be there on that first night when Clare fled to the little chapel called Portiuncula to become a *brother*, and much more.

Available from most booksellers or through Paraclete Press
www.paracletepress.com
1-800-451-5006
Try your local bookstore first.